ALEXANDER HAMILTON

The Making of America

★ TERI KANEFIELD ★

Abrams Books for Young Readers
New York

For Sabrina

TITLE PAGE: *Alexander Hamilton*, 1806, by John Trumbull.

Cataloging-in-Publication Data has been applied for and may be obtained from the Library of Congress.

ISBN: 978-1-4197-2578-4

Text copyright © 2017 Teri Kanefield

Book design by Sara Corbett

Printed and bound in U.S.A.

10 9 8 7 6 5 4 3 2

ABRAMS The Art of Books
115 West 18th Street, New York, NY 10011
abramsbooks.com

CONTENTS

Alexander Hamilton and Aaron Burr duel, 1870s engraving, artist unknown.

The Duel

O n a mild summer morning just after dawn, two men met on the dueling grounds in Weehawken, New Jersey. They were armed with Wodgon dueling pistols—heavy, elegant flintlock pistols, with highly polished curved wooden handles and brass barrels almost eleven inches long. One of the men was Aaron Burr, vice president of the United States. The other was former United States Secretary of the Treasury Alexander Hamilton. The year was 1804.

A few weeks earlier, Burr had demanded that Hamilton apologize for fifteen years of insults. When Hamilton refused, Burr challenged him to a duel—and Hamilton accepted.

Hamilton declined to practice before their meeting, even though he probably hadn't fired a pistol since the Revolutionary War. During the days leading up to the duel, he'd spent time getting his affairs in order, writing farewell letters and redrafting his will. On his writing desk, he left a lengthy declaration containing the statement: "I have resolved . . . to throw away my first fire, and I have thought even of reserving my second fire—and thus giving a double opportunity to Burr to pause and reflect." He'd also said this to a friend, who begged him not to squander his first shot. But Hamilton had made up his mind, and he was nothing if not stubborn and determined. "Then sir," his friend reportedly cried. "You will go like a lamb to be slaughtered."

According to the standards of the day, turning down a duel was the sign of a coward. It was also taken as evidence that the person declining was not a true gentleman and had indeed behaved dishonorably. But duels were against the law, and Hamilton would have had good reasons for refusing. He believed duels were sinful and wrong. His own beloved son Philip had recently died in a duel defending Hamilton's honor, and his death devastated his family. Hamilton knew that his own death would further traumatize them. Before leaving for the dueling field, he left behind a letter to his wife, Eliza, that read:

> If it had been possible for me to have avoided the interview, my love for you and my precious children would have been alone a decisive motive. But it was not possible, without sacrifices which would have rendered me unworthy of your esteem . . . Adieu best of wives and best of women.

In the papers Hamilton left behind, he admitted that Burr was justified in challenging him because he had, indeed, smeared Burr's character. But Hamilton couldn't avert the duel by apologizing because, in his opinion, everything he said was true.

Generations since have wondered about Hamilton's decision to accept Burr's challenge—and his decision to throw away his fire. Some suggested it was a death wish, as indicated by a letter he'd written in 1800, moaning that he should "withdraw from the scene. Every day proves to me more and more that this American world was not made for me." Others suggested that Hamilton, who had been frail all his life and over the past few years had suffered stomach disorders and other illnesses, believed himself to be dying anyway. It's also possible that Hamilton didn't believe Burr would shoot to kill. Duels, while sometimes fatal, more often were not fought to the death, instead stopping before shots were even fired, or at the first draw of blood, or after a few misfires.

Hamilton must have known that if Burr killed him, Burr would be committing political suicide because there'd be almost no chance he'd ever again hold public office. Perhaps Hamilton thought reason would prevail, that the ever-ambitious Burr, not wanting to entirely end his own career, would make a show of firing, content to inflict a wound, but stop short of killing him. There was another possibility. Hamilton had long romanticized a glorious death, so perhaps—knowing Burr would be committing political suicide by killing him—Hamilton thought it honorable to take a bullet to save the country from the threat posed by Burr.

★ ★ ★ ★ ★ ★ ★ ★ ★ ★ ★ ★ ★ ★ ★

Burr and Hamilton measured the distance of ten paces between them. Next they loaded their pistols and turned to face each other. Several others were there to watch and supervise, including two New York lawyers, Nathaniel Pendleton and

William Van Ness. Also present, as customary at duels, was a doctor.

Pendleton made sure both men were ready, then gave the signal by saying, "Present." Hamilton fired first, aiming upward. His bullet tore through the foliage overhead. Burr, who fired a moment later, aimed directly at Hamilton and shot him in the stomach. Hamilton fell to the ground. The doctor flew to his side. Hamilton looked up and said, "This is a mortal wound, Doctor." With that, he sank into unconsciousness.

Pendleton and the doctor lifted him up and carried him down to the riverbank, where a boatman waited. They'd rowed halfway across the Hudson River on their way back to Manhattan when Hamilton revived, his eyes fluttering but not opening all the way. He said his vision was blurred. He asked that the news be broken to his wife as gently as possible.

Hamilton died at home the next afternoon, surrounded by his wife and his children—leaving behind a nation shocked and angry, and a legacy that continues to this day.

1

An Orphan and a Dreamer

My ambition is prevalent that I contemn the groveling and condition of a clerk or the like to which my fortune condemns me and I would willingly risk my life though not my character to exalt my station.

— Alexander Hamilton

lex Hamilton was born in 1755 in Charleston on the island of Nevis in the British West Indies, a place of lush tropical jungles and sugar plantations. The island was only five miles across, surrounded by the sparkling turquoise waters of the Caribbean. Pirates swarmed the nearby seas. As a young boy, Alex would have seen captured pirates hauled through town to the courthouse for judgment before being hanged at Gallows Bay. He would have seen slaves brutally whipped in the open markets and sold in the auction blocks at

Market Shop and Crosses Alley. He would have seen trading ships from all over the world sail into Charleston's port.

He lived with his parents and his brother, James, who was two years older, in a humble stone house on the main street in Charleston, within sight of the beach. His father, James Hamilton, was something of a drifter. James was a younger son of a Scottish landowner whose family traced its lineage to the fourteenth century. The Hamiltons' ancestral home, a castle called the Grange, was located in Kilmarnock, Scotland. James came to the sugar islands to make his fortune. Getting started in the sugar trade was difficult, and unfortunately, James Hamilton had no head for business. Before long, he fell into debt.

Lacking the money for boat passage back to Scotland, he spent a few years in and out of jobs. He was working at the port when he met Rachel Fawcett, Alex's mother. Her father was a French Huguenot who had been driven from France because of his religion, and her mother was an Englishwoman. For a while, they had prospered, even owning a small sugar plantation in the foothills, before losing almost everything when a drought killed off a year's worth of crops.

Alex was slender, with reddish-brown hair, dark blue eyes, and the kind of pale, translucent skin that flushes easily. He never went to school. He learned French from his mother, and probably how to read and write from her as well. He was also tutored by an elderly Jewish woman, who taught him, among other things, to recite the Ten Commandments in Hebrew when he was still so young that he had to stand on a table to be by her side.

When Alex was nine, his father's brother in Scotland developed ties to a West Indian shipping company and was able to arrange a job for Alex's father. To take this new position, James Hamilton moved his family to the bustling seaport town of Christiansted on the larger island of

The Port of Christiansted, in the mid-eighteenth century, by H. G. Beenfeldt. This was the main port of St. Croix during Alexander Hamilton's childhood.

An Orphan and a Dreamer

St. Croix, a town consisting of warehouses, stores, shipping posts, a church, and a fort that was used as a prison.

After arriving in Christiansted, Alex learned that his mother had a secret: She was married to another man. On Nevis, his mother had been able to pass herself off as Mrs. Hamilton. That was no longer possible after the family moved because it was on St. Croix that Rachel had been married to someone else—and imprisoned.

Rachel was a girl of sixteen when she married John Michael Lavien, who was about thirty at the time.

She didn't want to marry him but gave in to the urging of her mother, who mistakenly believed that Lavien was a man of wealth. In fact, Lavien was the opposite; he peddled dry goods, hoping to advance himself into the planter class. He wanted to marry Rachel because at that time, her family still owned the small plantation.

Rachel came to hate her husband, who Alex later described as crude and overbearing. A year after they were married, they had a child, Peter. After a bitter falling-out, Lavien publicly accused Rachel of having affairs with other men and had her imprisoned for several months, thinking that imprisonment would turn her into the meek and obedient wife he wanted. When she was released from prison, instead of returning to her husband, she fled to Nevis, where she met Alex's father. By the time she returned to St. Croix with James Hamilton and their two sons, her oldest child, Peter, who was then about nineteen years old, had gone to live in South Carolina. Lavien had moved to the other side of the island, from Christiansted to Frederiksted.

About a year after Alex and his family moved to St. Croix, Alex's father scored his first business success: He managed to collect a large debt owed to the company he worked for. Shortly afterward, he deserted his family forever, leaving Rachel to care for their two boys.

He went to the nearby island of St. Kitts. Soon the money he'd earned was gone. He drifted farther south, where he lived out the rest of his life in poverty. Alex's view of his father was that he was lazy and not particularly competent, and that he deserted his family because he knew he could not support them. Over the years, Alex and his father occasionally exchanged letters, and later Alex offered him money, but they never saw each other again.

Society was highly stratified in the West Indies during Alex's youth. At the top were the wealthy planters, who carried themselves like European aristocrats, riding through town in fancy carriages and wearing expensive clothing, while back home on their plantations, hundreds of enslaved people toiled in the canebrakes—often naked—in the blistering hot sun. Just below the wealthy planters on the social hierarchy came the successful merchants and traders. Then came the craftsmen and laborers. Alex and his family were near the bottom of the hierarchy, just above the pickpockets, thieves, and drifters who roamed the streets of Christiansted. His status as a child born outside of marriage— declared illegitimate—whose father had abandoned him bumped him even further down the social ladder. His illegitimacy became a lifelong source of embarrassment.

After Alex's father left, Rachel rented a two-story house at 36 Company Street from a New York merchant, Nicholas Cruger, and opened a store on the ground floor. She kept her accounts in order and made all payments in a timely manner. The profits from her store enabled her to feed the family. From her parents, Rachel had inherited three women slaves, Flora, Rebecca, and Esther, who had four children among them. Soon she acquired two more adult female slaves and earned extra income by hiring them out.

Then came a series of tragedies. In February 1768, Rachel fell ill with a fever. About a week after she became sick, Alex came down with the same illness. Alex regained his health, but his mother didn't. She died at nine o'clock in the evening on February 19, 1768. Shortly afterward, the court seized all her money and possessions. Because Alex and his brother, James, were illegitimate, they were not permitted to inherit anything from her.

By this time, Rachel had almost no family. Her only living relatives were her deceased sister's husband, James Lytton, and his children, Alex's cousins, now grown to adulthood. For a while, Lytton had been the successful owner of a small sugar plantation. He still retained some of the wealth he had earned as a planter.

The court appointed Peter Lytton, James's son, as guardian to Alex and his brother, and held an auction to sell off Rachel's personal possessions, including her enslaved women and their children. James Lytton bought Rachel's books at the auction and gave them back to Alex. The proceeds from the auction were turned over to Peter Lavien, Rachel's oldest son, who was then a twenty-two-year-old churchwarden in South Carolina. He had made the trip back to the island to claim his inheritance. He snubbed his younger half-brothers and offered them nothing.

Alex and his brother went to live with Peter Lytton. At about this time, Alex went to work as a clerk for Beekman and Cruger, the New York trading company from which his mother had purchased goods for her store. He became chums with Edward Stevens, the son of a successful merchant. The friendship would last until the end of Alex's life.

Peter Lytton turned out to be mentally unstable. Within a few months of taking the boys into his home, he committed suicide, stabbing himself while lying in bed. His will left everything he owned to the child of his black mistress.

James Lytton died a few weeks later. Though the sugar islands were regularly plagued by a range of tropical diseases, including malaria, yellow fever, and dysentery, so many deaths in such a short time was horrifying and devastating. If all that had happened wasn't enough of a shock, it turned out that James Lytton had revised his will a mere five days earlier . . . and he also left nothing to Alex and his brother.

Fourteen-year-old Alex and his sixteen-year-old brother now had to fend for themselves. They went separate ways. James became a carpenter's apprentice and went to live with his new master. Alex went to live with the family of his pal Edward Stevens. It would become a pattern in his life that well-to-do, aristocratic families took to Alex, inviting them into their homes and their lives.

Not long after Alex went to live with the Stevens family, Edward, who was a year older than Alex, departed for New York to study medicine. Edward hoped to return to St. Croix and treat patients who suffered from the island's rampant diseases. Alex, who had to work for a living, remained in Christiansted as a clerk for Beekman and Cruger.

★ ★ ★ ★ ★ ★ ★ ★ ★ ★ ★ ★ ★ ★ ★

Alex felt stung by the injustices he had suffered. He resented the law that disinherited him because his parents hadn't been married. He hated the fact that a person's place in society came from birthright instead of ability and hard work. Taking stock of his own life, he feared that however hard he might work and however capable he might be, he'd rise no higher than a clerk. He longed for fame. He wished for a war so he could win respect on the battlefield and become a hero—the only way he could imagine earning a high place in society through his own accomplishments. He wrote passionate poetry, and he spun fantasies of glory and greatness.

Highly intelligent and quick to learn, he advanced rapidly at Beekman and Cruger. Soon he was doing managerial and accounting work. Because sugar prices were so high in Europe, the West Indies provided four-fifths of Great Britain's overseas wealth, far more than the thirteen North American colonies combined. Alex thus found himself working in a hub of international trade. He learned about all aspects of the shipping and trading markets. He became versed in finance and international commerce. He also learned about smugglers, and the need for a business to have access to credit. He came to understand the value of a uniform currency.

The company traded mostly in foodstuffs and dry goods, but they also handled an occasional shipment of enslaved men and women. By this time, Alex had grown to despise the slave trade,

Detail of the front page of the *Royal Danish American Gazette,* Danish West Indies, 1771.

which represented everything he hated about a stratified culture in which a person's destiny was determined by the circumstances of his or her birth.

Alex was fifteen when the *Royal Danish American Gazette* began publishing a paper on the island. It included poetry. Alex wrote a love poem and sent it to the editor with a letter, which read:

I am a youth about seventeen, and consequently such an attempt as this must be presumptuous; but if, upon perusal, you think the following piece worthy of a place in your paper, by inserting it you'll much oblige,
Your obedient servant, A.H.

While he gave his age as "about seventeen," he had, in fact, just turned sixteen. His poem appeared in the following issue. A Presbyterian minister named Hugh Knox, whose work was also published in the *Royal Danish American Gazette*, was so impressed with Alex's poem that he sought him out and befriended him. Knox made his library available to Alex and encouraged him to study.

The following year, in October 1771, Nicholas Cruger was forced to spend five months in New York because of his poor health. He designated Alex as the person to run the business in his absence—a big job for a sixteen-year-old. For five months, Alex made all the day-to-day decisions in a multinational trading firm. He collected money owed to the company. He inspected the goods and negotiated on behalf of the firm. He dealt with dishonest sea captains. He gambled on market prices. Written records and letters in his hand from this period show maturity well beyond his years. The experience fueled his dream that he was destined for something more.

✳ ✳ ✳ ✳ ✳ ✳ ✳ ✳ ✳ ✳ ✳ ✳ ✳ ✳ ✳

On the night of August 31, 1772, came the event that would, in a roundabout way, forever change young Alex's fortunes. That was the night a devastating hurricane struck St. Croix. For six hours, furious winds pounded the island, smashing homes, uprooting trees, tossing barrels of sugar and pieces of furniture as if they were weightless. The sea rose about twelve feet. Boats were flung onto the shore.

When the winds subsided, a shocked and dazed Alex wrote a letter to his father, describing the hurricane:

The roaring of the sea and wind, fiery meteors flying about in the air, the prodigious glare of almost perpetual lightning, the crash of the falling houses, and the ear-piercing shrieks of the distressed were sufficient to strike astonishment into Angels.

But then, Alex continued, God took mercy and relented:

He hears our prayer. The lightning ceases. The winds are appeased. The warring elements are reconciled and all things promise peace . . . Look back Oh! my soul, look back and tremble. Rejoice at thy deliverance, and humble thyself in the presence of thy deliverer.

The letter went on to describe the joy and relief—and humility—of the survivors. Alex showed the letter to Knox, who encouraged him to publish it. Alex hesitated, not wanting to capitalize on a tragedy. Knox prevailed, and the letter was published in the *Royal Danish American Gazette* on October 3, 1772. Immediately Alex became a literary sensation. Even the island's governor praised the letter and wanted to know more about the author. When the word went around that the letter was written by a motherless, illegitimate seventeen-year-old who'd received no formal education, Alex had his first taste of fame. Knox seized the moment and suggested to the island's elite that a young man with such promise should not go to waste on ledgers and accounts. He set up a fund to collect money to send Alex to North America for a real college education. The fund provided Alex with a stipend that he would collect regularly from Beekman and Cruger's New York offices.

Because the storm made it possible for Alex to come to the North American colonies for his education, it has been quipped that a hurricane blew him northward. Alex boarded a ship bound for Boston in the port of Christiansted, leaving behind a painful childhood filled with death, poverty, and the humiliation of a mother who had been publicly accused of infidelity and a father who deserted his family. He turned his eyes to the north. He never looked back, never longed for his boyhood home, and never returned to the islands.

2

An Immigrant

There are strong minds in every walk of life that will rise superior to the disadvantages of a situation, and will command the tribute due to their merit, not only from the classes to which they particularly belong, but from the society in general. The door ought to be equally open to all.

— Alexander Hamilton

The crossing of the sea was uneventful . . . until just off the coast of Massachusetts, where Alex's ship caught fire. The crew quickly extinguished the flames, but the brig, badly damaged, limped into Boston Harbor. It was, perhaps, an omen. Alex's life in North America would be dramatic and adventurous.

Shortly after arriving in Boston, Alex journeyed to New York and presented himself at the offices of Cruger's shipping company to collect his allowance. There he met Hercules Mulligan,

View of New York, 1794, by Archibald Robertson.

the younger brother of one of the firm's partners—and a member of the Sons of Liberty, a secret group dedicated to American independence. Hercules, who ran a tailor and haberdasher shop on Water Street, offered Alex a place to stay for a few days. Alex also met up with his chum from St. Croix, Edward Stevens, who was then a student at King's College in New York (now known as Columbia University).

Alex fell in love with New York City. It was already the second largest city in the colonies, behind Philadelphia and edging out

Boston. Founded by the Dutch West India Company in 1623 as an outpost, New York had always welcomed businesses. By the time Alex arrived, the city was a major trading center among the thirteen colonies, with attractive shops, counting houses, and a variety of businesses, including newspaper publishers. Merchants and traders had already begun to gather around Wall Street. Unlike New England, New York welcomed non-English-speaking immigrants and had thus become a vibrant and diverse cultural center. When Alex arrived, fourteen languages were spoken in the city. He admired the commercialized city as a place of opportunity for newcomers and the poor.

Alex carried letters of introduction from Knox to the most prominent figures in New York and New Jersey. As a result of

John Jay, date unknown, based on a painting by Gilbert Stuart.

Knox's connections, Alex was a frequent guest at Liberty Hall, the New Jersey home of William Livingston, a member of both Continental Congresses and later a signer of the Constitution. Alex spent time with the Boudinot family, getting to know Elias

Boudinot, a New Jersey lawyer who later served as president of the Congress. He became acquainted with John Jay, who became a New York delegate to the Continental Congress. Considered handsome, with boyish but finely chiseled features, Alex moved easily in the upper circles of society, dressing smartly in a long coat and white shirts with lace cuffs, his hair pulled back and tied with a black ribbon, in keeping with the style of the day—entirely looking the part of a well-bred young gentleman.

He was outgoing and gregarious, a good conversationalist who struck others as forthcoming and open—but there was much he concealed. He glossed over his childhood and family circumstances, avoiding the subject when he could, twisting the truth and implying that his parents had been married and that his father was the son of a Scottish nobleman when he couldn't.

At about this time, he shaved two years off his life, giving his birth year as 1757 instead of 1755 to hide the fact that he was late starting his education. Young men from good families generally began college at about fifteen. Frail and slight, with pale skin, narrow shoulders, and a tiny waist, he easily passed himself off as younger than he actually was.

The year was 1773, and the colonies were in turmoil. Most of Alex's new friends were strongly critical of Britain's rule over the colonies. Some, like Hercules Mulligan, were in favor of full rebellion. Others wanted to be fully integrated into the British Empire and to have the rights of citizens instead of mere colonists expected to do nothing more than send wealth back to Britain.

Alex, though, had little time for politics. He had a task: to acquire a college education. He planned to enter the College of New Jersey (later, Princeton University), a place known to be anti-British and pro-Patriot. Passing the entrance exam required mastery of French literature, English composition and literature, and mathematics; the ability to write in Latin; and the ability to translate Latin and Greek classics into English. While Alex was fluent in French from his mother, he didn't know a word of Latin or Greek. On Knox's recommendation, he enrolled at a preparatory academy run by a Princeton graduate, Francis Barber. The academy was located in Elizabethtown, New Jersey (now known as Elizabeth)—a charming village with windmills, two churches, and well-tended orchards.

The preparatory work Alex needed ordinarily required at least two years, but Alex threw himself into his studies with passion, studying late by candlelight and rising early for more lessons. In less than a year, he was ready for his exam. The president of Princeton, Rev. Dr. John Witherspoon, administered Alex's exam in a little study in the back of his house. He was impressed and declared Alex ready for college.

Alex wanted to earn his degree quickly, so he asked Witherspoon for permission to move at his own pace rather than follow the university's formal program. When Witherspoon refused, Alex applied to Columbia University, a university with Loyalist leanings. He preferred Princeton, but he was a young man in a hurry. The president of Columbia was Myles Cooper, a pro-British Loyalist who believed the colonies should remain part of the empire. Cooper agreed to Alex's unusual request. So in late 1773 or early 1774, Alex joined Edward Stevens at Columbia. His goal, like Edward's, was to become a doctor. He studied nonstop with the goal of graduating in two years.

King's College (Columbia), 1776, artist unknown.

Columbia then consisted of three faculty members and about twenty students housed in a large building. The campus was heavily wooded, located in what was then the northernmost reaches of the inhabited part of New York City. Alex joined a debating club and a literary society. He developed the eccentric habit of talking aloud to himself as he walked, rehearsing lessons or composing treatises.

He published his first political treatise, a thirty-five-page pamphlet entitled "A Full Vindication of the Measures of the Congress," on December 15, 1774. Like most political essayists of the time, he published anonymously. He signed his pamphlet "A Friend to America" and wrote that the British were "enemies to the natural rights of mankind . . . because they wish to see one part of their species enslaved by another." He encouraged colonists to "repel this atrocious invasion of our rights."

There were many people, including Columbia college president Cooper, who believed that the colonists would never be able to defeat the British Empire. Alex refuted these ideas in another pamphlet, predicting that the French and Spanish would enter the war on the side of the colonies. He also accurately predicted how the war with Britain would be fought and won:

Let it be remembered that there are no large plains for the two armies to meet in, and decide the contest by some decisive stroke . . . The circumstances of our country put it in our power to evade a pitched battle. It will be better policy to harass and exhaust the soldiery by frequent skirmishes and incursions than to take the open field with them, by which means they would have the full benefit of their superior regularity and skill.

When the rumor went around that "A Full Vindication of the Measures of the Congress" and the essays following had been written by a young college student, many didn't believe it. Some thought John Jay was the author. The essays were widely seen as every bit as sophisticated as the writings of Thomas Jefferson, who was then in his early thirties. Even Myles Cooper denied that one so young as Alex could have written the essays.

Alex mentioned death and martyrdom so often in his essays, letters, and poems that he seemed to have almost a death fixation, frequently glorifying a martyr's death. In urging the colonists to fight for liberty, he told them to "lead an honorable life or to meet with resignation a glorious death." He ended an essay with an allusion to Homer's *Iliad*: "Death is the worst, a fate which all must try; And, for our country, 'tis a bliss to die." And from his hurricane letter: "Death comes rushing on in triumph veiled in a mantle of tenfold darkness. His unrelenting scythe, pointed, and ready for the stroke."

Alex also had a gloomy view of humankind, saying, for example, that to expect a person with too much power to rule with kindness was to ignore history and the "degenerate" nature of the "race of mortals." Despite such a dark view of humanity, he was extraordinarily sympathetic to the suffering of others. When Elias Boudinot's infant daughter died, he stayed up all night with the grieving parents, and wrote a stirring and heartfelt eulogy. All through his studies, and later the war, he never stopped writing poetry. One thing was clear: Alex's feelings, like his intellect, ran deep.

✶ ✶ ✶ ✶ ✶ ✶ ✶ ✶ ✶ ✶ ✶ ✶ ✶ ✶ ✶

On December 20, 1773, Alex's life changed forever. That was the night Paul Revere—an express rider hired by the Boston Committee of Correspondence and the Massachusetts Committee of Safety to carry important messages—galloped into New York City with astonishing news of colonial defiance.

To protest the Tea Act, a band of the Sons of Liberty disguised as Indians had boarded British ships, and within three hours dumped more than ninety thousand pounds of tea into Boston Harbor. New York erupted into a furious whirlwind of rallies, protests, and speeches as New Yorkers debated whether to follow the example of the Bostonians.

THE TEA ACT was one of a series of regulations imposed by Britain on the colonies. The regulation, designed to save the East India Company from bankruptcy, granted the company a monopoly on importing tea to the colonies. The act ignited fury among the colonists, who resented Britain's attempts to force them to buy tea from British companies.

The colonies were on the brink of war, so Alex pulled himself away from his books to attend speeches and rallies. He made his debut on a political stage at a public meeting organized by the Sons of Liberty. In the midst of the crowds on a commons not far from the college, he waited for the right moment to leap onto the platform. Once on the stage, he urged the crowd to embrace North American liberty and reject "fraud, power, and the most odious oppression." When he stopped speaking, the crowd stood transfixed and amazed, marveling at the youth who spoke with such emotion and eloquence.

Alex had once wished for a war so he could prove himself a hero. In April, his wish came true. British Parliament declared Massachusetts in a state of rebellion. King George ordered his army to quash the insurgence. In Massachusetts, a skirmish later called the Battle of Lexington and Concord broke out between British soldiers and a motley Patriot militia called the minutemen, a band of civilians who boasted they could be ready to fight in a minute's notice. While Hamilton had foreseen this type of warfare, the British were shocked and scandalized. Instead of meeting face to face in an open battlefield, following accepted rules of warfare, the colonists hid behind walls and trees, ambushing the British with hit-and-run tactics.

While the Battles of Lexington and Concord proved indecisive, with both sides suffering losses, one thing was clear: The Patriots could stand up to the most powerful empire in the world. The Revolutionary War had begun.

Alex read books about infantry drills and military tactics, learning the art of war as eagerly as he'd learned to translate Greek and Latin. He joined a volunteer militia under the command of Captain Edward Fleming, a group that proudly donned green jackets and brown leather caps stitched with the motto "Liberty or Death." Small and lithe, Alex moved with grace and confidence. The military rolls listed the militia's name as the Corsicans, but they called themselves the Hearts of Oak. Each morning before classes, Alex and the other volunteers practiced drills in St. George's Courtyard. He followed political developments closely and took to writing letters to men in power, offering advice.

One night an angry mob of about four hundred men, enraged by Columbia president Myles Cooper's Loyalist views, pounded on the gates of the college. Alex and a friend rushed to Cooper's defense. Alex confronted the mob, risking his life as he tried to calm the angry men with a speech, imploring them not to disgrace a noble cause by attacking a defenseless citizen. Meanwhile, another student spirited Cooper away through the back alleys to a house where he could take refuge. From there Cooper boarded a British warship and set sail for England.

Not long afterward, when an angry group of Patriots tried to destroy the printing press of the leading Loyalist newspaper in New York, Alex wrote to John Jay suggesting that a law should be passed against such raids on private citizens. "In times of such commotion as the present," he wrote, "while the passions of men are worked up to an uncommon pitch there is great danger of fatal extremes." He urged Jay to take the steps necessary to "keep men steady and within proper bounds."

Alex had his first taste of war when a British warship, the *Asia,* entered New York Harbor. The leaders of the colony worried that the British might seize the cannons positioned at the tip of the Battery. Hamilton and a group of friends volunteered to remove the cannons under cloak of night. They'd moved most of the cannons northward to safety when the British saw what they were up to and fired at them. Alex and other members of his militia fired back. They then realized that they'd left behind one cannon. Alex ventured back to get it, braving the oncoming fire of the British. One of Alex's contemporaries reported that he seemed to have no fear of death.

3

A Soldier

*That Americans are entitled
to freedom is incontestable
upon every rational principle.*

— Alexander Hamilton

On July 2, 1776, the Second Continental Congress in Philadelphia voted in favor of independence. The delegates spent several days revising the Declaration of Independence, which they adopted on July 4. The next day, the declaration was printed in a shop in Philadelphia, and copies were dispatched to the thirteen colonies. Meanwhile, Admiral William Howe was preparing to unleash the full force of the Royal Navy—the mightiest in the world—against the colonists to crush the rebellion. General Howe, in command of a British fleet, landed on Staten Island, just across the harbor from New York City. He was joined by British ships from Lower New York Bay, bringing his total force to three hundred ships and 32,000 troops. Tensions in New York City ran high.

Knowing the city would soon be invaded, Alex left college to enlist full-time in New York's militia. He informed Knox and the others on the island of St. Croix who had contributed to his education by publishing a letter in the *Royal Danish American Gazette*, evoking the possibility of a hero's death in the service of his new country:

> I am going into the army and perhaps ere long may be destined to seal with my blood the sentiments defended by my pen. Be it so, if heaven decree it. I was born to die and my reason and conscience tell me it is impossible to die in a better or more important cause.

When the colony of New York formed an artillery company, Alex wanted to be in command. Having run a multinational shipping and trading company, he felt perfectly qualified, despite his youth. Several of his highly placed friends agreed and pooled their influence behind him.

He was commissioned as a captain on the condition that he

Alexander Hamilton
in the Uniform of the
New York Artillery, 1857,
by Alonzo Chappel.

enlist thirty men. He and his friend Hercules Mulligan enlisted twenty-five the first day. Soon they had sixty-eight. Alex threw himself into organizing, training, and disciplining his troops, using knowledge gleaned from the books he'd read on warfare. He wrote letters asking for an increase in pay for his men to make it easier to recruit new soldiers, and he wrote letters to secure proper uniforms. Always careful about his own appearance, he believed that solders must be dressed smartly if they were to perform like professionals. He got everything he asked for, outfitting his men in dashing blue coats, buckskin trousers, and white belts crisscrossing their chests.

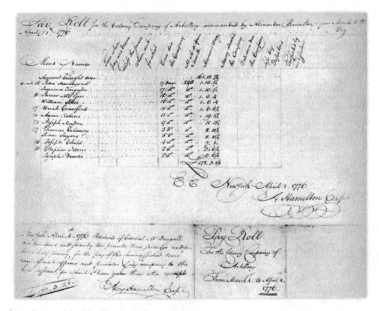

Payroll record for Hamilton's artillery company.

His administrative skills came to the attention of Brigadier General William Alexander, known as Lord Stirling, who wanted Alex to become his aide-de-camp, the term for a high-ranking military officer who acts as a confidential assistant to a senior officer. Alex refused. The last thing he wanted was a dull desk job, which would feel like being a clerk again and groveling to someone else. He wanted action, glory, and rapid advancement. It was rumored that another general, Nathanael Greene, also asked Alex to become his aide.

Several battles were fought in New York that summer and fall. During the Battle of Harlem Heights, Alex and his men fought alongside General George Washington. The Continental Army, outnumbered and outmaneuvered, suffered devastating losses. Alex and his men were with Washington when, badly beaten, he withdrew the weary Continental Army across New Jersey toward Philadelphia. They abandoned New York City to the British, leaving many New Yorkers convinced that the British were invincible.

There are differing accounts as to when Washington first became aware of Alex. One historian suggested that General Greene told Washington about him. According to another report, while preparing for the Battle of Harlem Heights, Washington first noticed Alex's organizational talents as he watched him supervise the building of an earthen embankment.

On January 20, 1777, General Washington asked Alex to serve as one of his personal aides-de-camp with a promotion to lieutenant colonel. While Alex wanted to be a war hero and didn't like the idea of being a subordinate or taking a desk job, he couldn't resist the promotion. It was, after all, no small thing to be aide-de-camp to General Washington himself, who was commander in chief of the entire Continental Army, and who was already an internationally known and widely respected figure. Besides, Washington made clear that his aides were expected to do more than relay orders. He required all his aides to be skilled writers, well educated, cultured, and intelligent, with "the soul of a general"—able to think for him, compose letters, and respond to emergencies with little or no direction.

George Washington was badly in need of administrative help. He was not only in command of the army; he had to act as a high-level diplomat, placating the new Congress and preventing individual states—who had yet to really pull together as a single nation—from becoming jealous of one another. He once remarked, "My time is so taken up at my desk that I am obliged to neglect many other essential parts of my duty; it is absolutely necessary . . . to have persons that can think for me, as well as execute orders."

Alex became one of a handful of Washington's aides-de-camp, who included such luminaries as the Marquis de Lafayette, a French aristocrat who came to fight on the side of the colonists. Washington referred to his aides as his military family. The aides shared a room for sleeping and a room for working. Friends and colleagues now referred to Alex by his last name. As the youngest of the aides-de-camp, the others nicknamed him "Ham" or "Hammie." He still looked so young that one observer described him as a boy. He and his fellow aides-de-camp developed a strong bond and sense of brotherhood and became lifelong friends. Many would play important roles in the building of the new nation.

Hamilton and Washington had complementary personalities. Washington was cool, aloof, and quiet, giving the impression of dignity, while in fact he felt awkward in social situations. He enjoyed the company of men like Hamilton, who were talkative and outgoing, prone to joking and warm camaraderie. While Hamilton pored over books and easily absorbed complex theories, Washington, a gifted military leader, didn't have the patience for philosophy. A man of action, Washington surrounded himself with thinkers and talkers.

The job of Washington's aide-de-camp was perfect for Hamilton, with his gift for letter writing, his speaking skills, his depth of knowledge, and his experience in international business. As one of Washington's right-hand men, he communicated regularly with the highest-ranking leaders of the new nation. He compiled intelligence reports based on information from released prisoners and exchanged twice-weekly reports with the leaders of New York about the progress of the army. He drew up a plan for reorganizing the army, drafted a set of new military regulations, and negotiated prisoner exchanges with the British. His native fluency in French allowed him to communicate with French soldiers who came to fight for America. He had no family to visit, so he lived at the army headquarters, never taking a day off. Soon he advanced to become something akin to Washington's chief of staff—in Washington's words, his "principal and most confidential aide."

Hamilton's position allowed him to see firsthand the workings and flaws of the new American government, including the political wrangling between the states. Things were not going well for the new nation or for the Continental Army. During the difficult winter of 1778 at Valley Forge, the army was underfed, insufficiently clothed, and worn down with fatigue and illness—2,500 soldiers died, and thousands more were without food, firewood, and shoes. Something had to be done if the bedraggled and starving army hoped to win a war against the British Empire.

Hamilton and John Laurens, one of his fellow aides-de-camp and closest friends, believed that if slaves were given their freedom in exchange for fighting for American independence, the army would at once have enough men to defeat the British. Laurens, the son of a wealthy and influential South Carolina planter, was an unlikely abolitionist. However, like Hamilton, he believed the institution of slavery was morally wrong, and he understood the hypocrisy of fighting for independence while enslaving a large portion of the population. Besides, as a practical matter, keeping what amounted to an army in slavery for personal profit while the enfeebled Continental Army starved was, to Hamilton, the height of folly.

Hamilton shocked many of his contemporaries by insisting that blacks were not naturally inferior to whites, but instead forced by circumstances into their present inferior status. If blacks were given proper training and the opportunity to fight, Hamilton had "not the least doubt that the Negroes will make very excellent soldiers." His idea that blacks were just as intelligent and capable as whites was radical at the time. Even his contemporaries who wanted to abolish slavery believed that blacks should be returned to Africa or sent elsewhere—perhaps to the West—to build their own communities.

The idea of freeing slaves to fight the British was not met with enthusiasm. Most of the resistance, not surprisingly, came from the southern plantation owners. Because of the cash value of tobacco, indigo, and rice, the southern colonies were the wealthiest in North America—their riches harvested by means of slave labor. The very idea of arming black men and teaching them to fight struck terror into the souls of southern landowners, who in some locations were significantly outnumbered by blacks, and who lived in fear of slave uprisings. Eventually about five thousand blacks—some of whom were already free, others who were granted freedom in exchange for joining the Continental Army—did fight alongside the Patriots, but rarely were they given combat duties or positions of responsibility.

✳ ✳ ✳ ✳ ✳ ✳ ✳ ✳ ✳ ✳ ✳ ✳ ✳ ✳ ✳

As soldiers starved to death at Valley Forge, Hamilton wrote passionate pleas to Congress for help. When Congress failed to act, Hamilton blamed the shortages on the ineptitude of the Articles of Confederation.

THE ARTICLES OF CONFEDERATION— a predecessor of the Constitution we have today—was the document written in 1777 that outlined America's first government. The new government established by the Articles had no president and no courts. The only federal government was the Continental Congress, which had almost no authority. The states were self-governing. The new nation was thus a loose confederation of sovereign states.

Because the federal government had no way to raise money, it had to scrape together the funds to pay the soldiers by begging for money from the states. The states were reluctant to send money to what seemed like a foreign government. They often kept their best soldiers and military strategists for their own militias as well.

It became clear to Hamilton that unless the states pulled together as a single country and formed a strong central government, they would lose the war. Even if they managed to win the war while in disarray, Hamilton could not see how a stable country could ever emerge from such chaos.

In a misguided attempt to solve its financial problems, Congress printed too much paper money, causing the value of the money to decline until it was almost worthless, which in turn ignited an economic crisis. American farmers often sold their crops to the British instead of to the Continental Army because they didn't trust American currency. Hamilton railed openly against Congress for being incompetent and unable to feed the troops at Valley Forge. He gave in to bouts of depression and despair, writing to John Laurens:

> The truth is I am an unlucky honest man, who speaks my sentiments to all and with emphasis. I say this to you because you know it and will not charge me with vanity. I hate Congress— I hate the army—I hate the world—I hate myself. The whole is a mass of fools and knaves.

George Washington, who had no children of his own, felt a particular fondness for Hamilton and treated him like a son. Washington was twenty-three years older than Hamilton, with a much larger build. Washington was steady and serene, a sharp contrast to the moody and emotional Hamilton. Hamilton found much to admire in Washington. While he was close enough to witness Washington's occasional bouts of temper, he saw that Washington was a brilliant general and effective leader. Hamilton approved of the way Washington managed his army. In European armies, as in European society in general, the aristocrats occupied the highest and most prestigious positions. Those of lower birth could rise only so high. Washington, in contrast, rewarded ability regardless of birth, which Hamilton viewed as fitting for a new nation that had declared all men created equal. Hamilton understood that because Washington chose his staff on the basis of merit, he—the illegitimate, immigrant son of a drifter— could rise to the position of chief of staff to General Washington himself.

In time, though, Hamilton grew impatient with his role of aide-de-camp. He longed for glory on the battlefield. He wanted to lift his sword and lead men into battle with colors flying, to the stirring sound of fifes and the pounding of drums. He believed that the military heroes of the revolution would be the ones to forge the new nation in peacetime, and he wanted to be among them. While Washington often let other aides-de-camp lead military commands, he continually refused to allow Hamilton to take a leading role on the battlefield. Washington believed that Hamilton was too valuable to him. He had plenty of people who could lead a charge against the British, but few with Hamilton's administrative and letter-writing talents.

Hamilton came to resent being consigned to a desk job. If he looked to Washington as a father figure, it wasn't always in a good way: He often resented Washington for not letting him do things he wanted to do.

To improve himself, and to prepare for a leadership role in the new government, Hamilton spent his spare time reading the great philosophers: Bacon, Hobbes, Cicero, and others. He read European history, including military history. He read *The Universal Dictionary of Trade and Commerce* by Malachy Postlethwayt, considered the most important book on trade and economics, a book that taught him the folly of printing too much paper money.

He read about politics, and considered the checks and balances that permitted personal freedom without allowing for the rise of a dictator. Like the other founders of the country, he absorbed the political theories of the English philosopher and physician John Locke, who famously said that government is a contract between the rulers and the ruled—that citizens exchange obedience for safety—but the contract is not binding. The government exists by consent of the governed. It was also John Locke who first said that *all* people have the right to life, liberty, and property. Inspired by his reading, Hamilton continued his habit of writing letters to men in power, offering advice.

He also took time to keep in touch with the important figures from his childhood. His buddy Edward Stevens had completed his medical training in Scotland and returned to St. Croix, where he became a highly respected doctor. Hamilton also corresponded with Hugh Knox, the minister who had made it possible for Hamilton to come to North America, and who continually expressed his personal pride in the man Hamilton had become. He exchanged letters on occasion with his brother, James, who was a carpenter in St. Croix, sending money when his brother needed it. He also tried to keep in touch with his father, but his father rarely responded. Hamilton assumed that his father kept his distance and remained silent because he was ashamed. Once, in a letter to his brother, after remarking on their father's silence, he said, "My heart bleeds at the recollection of his misfortunes and embarrassments."

4

Victory in Love and War

Before no mortal ever knew
A love like mine so tender, true
Completely wretched—you away,
And but half blessed even while you stay.

—Alexander Hamilton
to Eliza Schuyler

eorge Washington expected his aides-de-camp to devote themselves one hundred percent to their work, without distractions. "I give in to no kind of amusement myself," Washington said, "and consequently those about me can have none, but are confined from morning till eve, hearing and answering the applications and letters." But there *were* times of amusement: lulls in the fighting, particularly during the long winters, when Washington's aides could sneak in time for a little romance.

The wives of the officers and generals occasionally visited the camp, led by Martha Washington herself, often accompanied by their unmarried daughters. Washington chose not to play the host, instead assigning the task to his aides-de-camp. Thus there were dances and tea parties and opportunities for the aides-de-camp to flirt with the young ladies. Hamilton, who did nothing in half measures, earned the reputation of being girl-crazy. He became infatuated with one young lady after another. There was a good reason Martha Washington named her tomcat Hamilton. ("Tomcat" was a common term to describe a man who enjoyed pursuing women.)

Mrs. Washington has a tom-cat (which she calls in a complimentary way, Hamilton), with thirteen stripes around the tail, and its flaunting suggested the stripes for the flag.

Hamilton, outgoing and sociable, was the perfect host, refilling glasses, offering gallant toasts. One woman who visited the camp said he "acquitted himself with an ease, propriety and vivacity." A colonel from Pennsylvania described him as a "sensible genteel polite young fellow, a West Indian." General Greene described him as "a bright gleam of sunshine."

Then Hamilton met Elizabeth Schuyler. She was one of four

sisters, all known for their good humor and good looks, and he met several of them at once when he was on an errand in Albany, New York. He was invited to dine in the home of General Philip Schuyler.

The Schuyler family was one of the most influential and wealthiest in New York, having been granted manorial rights under the former Dutch governments of New York and New Jersey, granting them status similar to European nobility. The Schuyler estate extended three miles along the Hudson River. The Schuylers' wealth and prestige increased when Philip Schuyler married Catherine Van Rensselaer, who was heiress to a 120,000-acre estate in Columbia County in New York. Elizabeth, known to her friends and family as Betsey or Eliza, grew up in a household at the center of colonial influence. While she had no formal education—she was tutored at home, as was typical for girls at the time—she was well versed in politics and current affairs.

A painting of the Schuyler mansion in Albany, New York, 1818, by Philip Hooker.

She had been taught to play backgammon by none other than Benjamin Franklin, a frequent guest at the Schuyler mansion in Albany.

Little was written of the first meeting between Hamilton and Eliza, so we don't know their first impressions of each other. We do know that while Hamilton eagerly carried on flirtations during this period, he was not yet ready to marry. He'd told a friend that a soldier should remain unmarried, having no wife other than the military.

He changed his mind when he was twenty-four years old. The winter of 1779–80 was snowy and bitterly cold, even harsher than the previous winter at Valley Forge. The army was camped in Morristown, New Jersey. Hamilton was feeling depressed. Washington had allowed John Laurens to go on a combat mission, but required Hamilton to remain in the camp. His spirits were temporarily revived by a round of dancing parties and dinners attended by the wives and daughters of generals and officers.

On February 2, 1780, Eliza Schuyler arrived in Morristown with William Livingston's daughter, Kitty Livingston, another girl Hamilton had flirted with. The young women stayed with Eliza's uncle and aunt who lived in Morristown. Hamilton met Eliza for the second time when she attended a dancing assembly.

He took notice of her dark hair, lively dark eyes, and gentle manners. Soon afterward, when Hamilton announced to his friends that he'd fallen in love—this time for real—it's unlikely that they took him seriously. But he *was* serious. He took to spending every evening with Eliza at the home of her uncle and aunt. He wrote her poetry. He became absentminded. One evening he returned to headquarters so absorbed in thoughts of Eliza that he could not remember the code for entering. "Hamilton's a gone man," a fellow aide-de-camp reported.

Within a month, he proposed marriage, warning her not to accept him if she could not be content living in relative poverty, for he admitted to having nothing. She accepted his proposal, and they anxiously awaited permission from Eliza's parents to marry. It became clear to Hamilton's friends that the calm and steady Eliza was a good match for the sensitive and often moody Hamilton.

On April 8, 1780, Eliza's father wrote to Hamilton, saying that he and Eliza's mother accepted his proposal of marriage. It was a wonder to many that Philip Schuyler, who was notoriously snobby and class-conscious, welcomed into his family an immigrant without land or money who was rumored to be illegitimate. Presumably when Philip Schuyler looked into Hamilton's background, he was impressed that Hamilton had risen to become George Washington's most trusted aide and concluded that Hamilton's genius and charm outweighed a lack of family connections and social status. Perhaps, too, the Schuylers gave their approval because two of their daughters had recently eloped, and they were afraid of another runaway marriage, particularly because Eliza was as independently minded as her sisters. Once the engagement was announced, Mr. and Mrs. Schuyler came to Morristown and rented a house not far from the army camp. Each evening Hamilton was their guest.

Elizabeth Schuyler Hamilton, date and artist unknown.

As always, he had a gift for forming friendships and connections. He and the Schuylers bonded as a family. Hamilton and his soon-to-be father-in-law held the same political views. Both believed that the finances of the new nation and the Continental Army were in shambles because the Articles of Confederation weakened the central government. Both agreed that it was impossible for George Washington, while leading the army, to also carry out the duties that should be performed by a central government administration.

In July, after the Schuylers returned to Albany, the lovesick and lonely Hamilton wrote to Eliza:

J love you more and more every hour. The sweet softness and delicacy of your mind and manners, the elevation of your sentiments, the real goodness of your heart, its tenderness to me, the beauties of your face and person, your unpretending good sense and that innocent simplicity and frankness which pervade your actions; all these appear to me with increasing amiableness and place you in my estimation above all the rest of your sex.

Now more than ever, desiring to impress Eliza and the Schuylers, Hamilton longed for glory in battle. He begged Washington to let him join General Greene, who was then fighting the British in the South, but again Washington refused. In November, when there were rumors that the British were planning to attack upper Manhattan, he tried again, and again Washington refused.

As if this wasn't frustrating enough, twice Hamilton was nominated for important diplomatic posts, once as an envoy to

France to join Benjamin Franklin in promoting American causes, and once as an envoy to Russia. Twice Congress passed over him for others. John Laurens was sent as the envoy to France, even though Laurens insisted that Hamilton, who spoke French with native fluency, was better qualified. Hamilton believed he was not selected because of his low social status.

Meanwhile, the new nation's financial situation deteriorated even further. Paper money lost so much value that Congress tried to restore order by issuing one new dollar for forty old ones, wiping out the savings of many Americans. State governments were falling deeper into debt.

Hamilton spent his spare time reading financial treatises. He understood that the reason for the current inflation—money losing value while prices of goods skyrocketed—started with wartime shortages, but most of the problem came from lack of confidence in the strength of the American dollar, and the chaos of each state issuing its own currency. He studied the rise of powerful nations and saw a pattern: Countries prospered and became wealthy when their governments had access to wealth. The Dutch Republic, like the United States, started out as a part of a larger empire—the Spanish. The Dutch were able to gain true independence after figuring out how to stabilize the economy and fill their coffers with cash, which they did by setting up a national bank and borrowing money. The result was a Dutch financial revolution, which gave rise to the Dutch trading companies that colonized New York. Britain, following the example of the Dutch, set up the Bank of England, which in turn permitted Britain to become one of the wealthiest and most powerful countries on Earth.

Hamilton wrote letters to members of Congress setting forth a detailed program to rescue the new nation's finances from the downward spiral; it was a plan that included a central bank modeled on the Bank of England.

✶ ✶ ✶ ✶ ✶ ✶ ✶ ✶ ✶ ✶ ✶ ✶ ✶ ✶ ✶

On December 14, 1780, Hamilton and Eliza were married in the drawing room of the Schuyler mansion in Albany, a stately redbrick structure overlooking the river and well-tended grounds. The bride wore a fashionable white wig and her grandmother's lace veil. Hamilton wore a black velvet coat, white silk breeches, and stockings, his shoes sparkling with rhinestone buckles borrowed from a good friend and fellow aide, the Marquis de Lafayette. The couple had a brief honeymoon in Albany before Hamilton returned to Washington's headquarters.

✳ ✳ ✳ ✳ ✳ ✳ ✳ ✳ ✳ ✳ ✳ ✳ ✳ ✳ ✳

In early 1781, General John Sullivan wanted to nominate Hamilton for the position of superintendent of finances, a post newly created by the Continental Congress. What Hamilton probably didn't know was that Sullivan asked Washington's opinion of Hamilton's qualifications for the post, and Washington recommended him highly, saying, "[T]here are few men to be found, of his age, who have a more general knowledge than he possesses, and none whose soul is more firmly engaged in the cause, or who exceeds him in probity and sterling virtue." Despite this glowing recommendation, the post was given to Robert Morris.

On a cold afternoon in February not long after Washington gave such high praise of Hamilton, he asked to see Hamilton immediately. Hamilton sent word that he had a letter to deliver but would return shortly. On his way back, he stopped to chat with Lafayette. When he climbed the stairs, Washington was waiting for him at the top—and Washington was furious.

"Colonel Hamilton," he said, "you have kept me waiting at the head of the stairs these ten minutes . . . you treat me with disrespect."

Hamilton's response was equally abrupt—and startlingly

childish. "I am not conscious of it, sir, but since you have thought it necessary to tell me so, we part."

Washington responded with, "Very well, sir, if it be your choice."

Hamilton turned and went to the room he shared with the other aides-de-camp. About an hour later, Washington, showing he was far more mature than Hamilton, sent one of the aides to find Hamilton and give him a message: He had not intended to hurt Hamilton's feelings, and he wanted to make amends.

Hamilton, though, refused to budge. He'd decided to leave, and that was that. Because Washington was temporarily understaffed, Hamilton told Washington he would stay until he could be replaced. Two days later, Hamilton remained agitated. The reason he offered his friends and family for such a strong reaction to what was surely a trivial event was years of frustration at being chained to a desk. He wrote to Philip Schuyler, describing the confrontation on the stairs and protesting his innocence. He also insisted he would leave Washington's service and never return. Seeking his father-in-law's approval, he concluded his letter saying, "I wish what I have said to make no other impression than to satisfy you that I have not been in the wrong." His new father-in-law wrote back, advising Hamilton to patch things up for everyone's benefit, but Hamilton's mind was made up.

Hamilton assured Washington he would keep their quarrel private, but soon he was sending off letters, revealing that they'd had a falling-out. He wrote to General Greene asking for a job in the southern army. He sent other letters bursting with rage at Washington. In one, he wrote, "Without a shadow of reason and on the slightest ground, he charged me in the most affrontive manner with disrespect." When Washington learned that their quarrel was public, he became even more irritated with Hamilton. Lafayette tried but failed to reconcile them.

Hamilton continued in his duties for a few more weeks. Then, in March, Washington departed for his New Windsor headquarters, located about sixty miles north of Manhattan. Shortly afterward, Hamilton joined Eliza in the Schuyler mansion in Albany. Still hoping to secure a combat mission, he found lodging for himself and Eliza located conveniently just across the Hudson River from Washington's headquarters.

Hamilton spent the next few months reading books on commerce, finance, and political philosophy while trying to find a position for himself in the field. He applied to other generals and urged his former colleagues to press Washington to give him a combat mission. Meanwhile, sitting on the sidelines of the war, he wrestled with feelings of depression, discouragement, and resentment.

★ ★ ★ ★ ★ ★ ★ ★ ★ ★ ★ ★ ★ ★ ★

Over the summer, British General Charles Cornwallis invaded Virginia. Thomas Jefferson, then the governor of Virginia, fled for safety to the back country with members of the legislature—a move that would later allow his enemies, many of whom had fought in the war, to call him a coward. Cornwallis camped his forces of nine thousand men near Yorktown, in a region surrounded by water on three sides: the York River, the James River, and the Chesapeake Bay. Cornwallis, backed up by the powerful Royal Navy, believed the location was safe.

What Cornwallis didn't know was that—in a stroke of amazingly good luck for the Americans—a French fleet was just then heading to the Chesapeake Bay. Washington planned to use the French fleet to block Cornwallis's escape from Yorktown by sea while forces led by Lafayette, Count Rochambeau, and Washington himself, would block Cornwallis's escape by land. Cornwallis and his nine thousand men would be trapped. The Americans and their allies would be able to attack from all sides.

Victory in Love and War

On July 31, Tench Tilghman, one of Washington's aides-de-camp and Hamilton's good friend, brought Hamilton thrilling news: George Washington was putting Hamilton in charge of New York and Connecticut regiments.

Hamilton's orders were to take one of the British forts in the coming siege of Yorktown. Once Hamilton understood the nature of the mission, he must have known he would be leading a command in what might be the grand finale of the Revolutionary War.

Storming of Redoubt #10 During the Siege of Yorktown, 1909, by H. Charles McBarron,

★ ★ ★ ★ ★ ★ ★ ★ ★ ★ ★ ★ ★ ★ ★

O n October 14, 1781, Hamilton waited in the trenches with his troops. The night was moonless and dark. His battalion consisted of 320 men. The British fort, which they could see from their hiding place, had been created from a pair of powerful artillery emplacements dug into the earth, reinforced with a pile of cut trees, the sharpened limbs facing the Continental Army. Their watchword was "Rochambeau," French for "a good one," chosen in honor of the French general allied with the Continental Army and because it sounded like "rush on boys."

Some of the battalion had axes to clear away the emplacements. Hamilton and others were armed with bayonets. They'd unloaded their guns so as not to accidentally shoot and take away the element of surprise. At eight o'clock, three cannons fired in rapid succession—the signal Hamilton was waiting for. He led his battalion from the trenches to storm the British encampment. They had about five hundred yards to cross. It was impossible to approach the emplacements in complete silence. The sound of their approach alerted the British, who opened fire on Hamilton's men—some of whom were hit. The others continued charging.

Hamilton hoisted himself over the parapet by standing on the shoulders of a taller man. He was the first to enter, with others following. The fighting was brief, but bloody. Eight of Hamilton's men were killed and another thirty wounded. Within eight minutes, the Continental Army had taken the fort by force. At the same time, French regiments attacked and captured the other key British fort. Later, in a letter describing the siege, Hamilton bragged that his men, forgiving past slights, spared the life of every British soldier who ceased fighting.

During the siege, Cornwallis tried to retreat across the York River but was prevented by a midnight storm. American and French regiments continued assaulting the remaining British strongholds. On the morning of October 17, a teenaged British drummer appeared on one of the parapets. Nobody could hear him over the thunder of cannons and gunfire, but when an officer appeared behind him flapping a white handkerchief, the weapons fell silent. Cornwallis asked for a twenty-four-hour truce. Washington gave him two hours and demanded unconditional surrender. The next day, representatives from both sides met to work out the terms of Cornwallis's surrender.

The formal surrender ceremony was held in Yorktown. Cornwallis himself did not attend, claiming illness as his excuse. His second-in-command, General Charles O'Hara, carried

Cornwallis's sword and formally surrendered 7,087 officers and ground troops, nine hundred seamen, 144 cannons, and more than forty-five vessels. The British band played "The World Turned Upside Down."

Hamilton watched the ceremony, mounted on his horse. He was fatigued, but he got what he'd long wanted. He was a hero of the American Revolutionary War. When the ceremony was over and the band finished playing, his work was done. He was soon galloping off to Albany, where Eliza—who was then expecting their first child—awaited him.

The Surrender of Cornwallis at Yorktown, c. 1860, by Charles-Édouard Armand-Dumaresq.

5

Striving for Magnificence

*There is something noble and magnificent in
the perspective of a great Federal Republic, closely
linked in the pursuit of a common interest . . . but
there is something proportionally diminutive and
contemptible in the prospect of a number of
petty states . . . jarring, jealous, and perverse.*

— Alexander Hamilton

Hamilton arrived in Albany fatigued and ill from the strain of battle. He spent a few months resting at the Schuyler mansion. On January 22, 1782, his son Philip was born. He savored the quiet time with his family.

The victory at Yorktown did not formally end the war. The British continued to occupy certain areas, including New York City. But after Cornwallis's crushing defeat, the British no longer had the heart to keep fighting. Instead of retaliating, the British opened peace negotiations. There wasn't much left for a soldier to do, so in March, Hamilton officially resigned from the Continental Army.

What he needed now was a profession. He decided to become a lawyer as a way to provide for his family—and because it was the quickest route to a political career. There were no law schools yet, so the usual way to become a lawyer was to study as an apprentice with an established attorney. It was also customary for the apprentice to pay for the training, with the period of apprenticeship generally lasting three years. Such an arrangement worked fine when the aspiring lawyer had enough wealth to pay for the privilege of an apprenticeship, but with a wife and child to support, Hamilton couldn't afford it and didn't have time.

So he gave himself a crash course in law. His primary text was Blackstone's *Commentaries on the Laws of England*. While studying, he did what law students customarily do: He created his own outline of the law as a study tool, which he called *Practical Proceedings in the Supreme Court of the State of New York*, 177 pages of notes and legal forms he drafted himself. His outline was so thorough, law students who followed used it as a textbook. Hamilton prepared for the New York bar exam—the exam administered by the New York courts to determine whether a person is qualified to practice law—by memorizing the entire outline, which he did by pacing back and forth and repeating it aloud to himself until he could recite it all verbatim. Six months after he began studying, in July 1782, he passed the exam.

About that time, Robert Morris, superintendent of finance for the Continental Congress, offered Hamilton an official appointment: tax collector for New York, a job with the title of "continental receiver." His task was to collect the taxes that New York owed the federal government. Hamilton accepted the position, inspired by the deep conviction that the survival of the new country required money in the federal coffers.

The problem was that New York was close to bankruptcy and still burdened by the British occupation. New York City, once a hub of trade and commerce, had been reduced to half-ruined houses and rubbish-filled streets teeming with livestock. Most of the state consisted of farmers who could barely make ends meet. Nobody had a penny to spare.

After four months as a continental receiver, Hamilton resigned in frustration, completely discouraged by what he saw. During the war, the states had pulled together to defeat the British. Now that they believed they were competitors, each state tried to get ahead by taxing its neighbors, creating their own border patrols and imposing tariffs on one another as if each state was an independent country.

A TARIFF, also called a custom duty, is a tax paid on certain imports and exports. Tariffs are indirect taxes, meaning they are not imposed directly on the consumer; they are imposed on the goods themselves. As a practical matter, though, the consumer ultimately pays, because tariffs are added to the price of goods. The effect of states imposing tariffs on one another was that prices throughout the country became inflated.

New Jersey had its own custom service charged with the task of collecting duties on goods entering and leaving the state. Virginia penalized imports from other states. New York taxed produce from New Jersey and lumber from Connecticut. Connecticut and New Jersey accused New York of greed. States issued their own currency. As a result, America's finances sank even deeper into chaos.

The problem—in Hamilton's view—was that financial reform could not happen without political reform. Until America had a strong central government, the states' finances would remain in shambles. The states would be unable to pay off their war debts without trying to fleece their neighboring states. As a result, the nation would have no credibility abroad and would be unable to raise the capital to rebuild. It seemed obvious to Hamilton that the only way to save the new nation was to scrap the Articles of Confederation, which he called "constitutional imbecility," and write a whole new Constitution.

So when the New York legislature appointed Hamilton as a delegate to the Continental Congress for a one-year term, he seized the chance to help revive the economy and help America achieve its potential. He accepted the appointment, fully aware of the irony. For years he'd been railing against Congress, calling it feeble, incompetent, and inefficient—and now he was about to join the very governing body of which he had such a low opinion. He believed, however, the problems were largely structural, and that Congress was enfeebled because of the Articles of Confederation. He intended to fix the defects.

In November 1782, he set off on horseback from Albany to Philadelphia, feeling cautiously optimistic. He had fought to make America free. Now, as a congressional delegate, he would work to make America productive and happy. His hopes were given a boost by the fact that the Americans, British, and French had recently signed a preliminary peace treaty recognizing the United States of America as an independent country. Initially the British sought to make peace with each state individually, but John Jay, Benjamin Franklin, and John Adams—representing the United States—rejected the proposal and said the treaty must be signed by the United States as a single entity. This led Hamilton to believe that at last, the states were ready to pull together as a union.

✶ ✶ ✶ ✶ ✶ ✶ ✶ ✶ ✶ ✶ ✶ ✶ ✶ ✶ ✶

Congress met in the Assembly Room on the ground floor of the Pennsylvania State House, today known as Independence Hall—a Georgian-style brick building with a symmetrical facade, located on a pleasant tree-lined street. It was a dignified, two-story building, with scrolled pediments over the doorways and ornamental woodwork lining the interior walls. While Congress was in session, the shades were kept down to block the outside noise, and for privacy. The congressional delegates sat in straight-backed Windsor chairs at tables covered with green or burgundy fabric edged with gold fringe.

Striving for Magnificence

Hamilton found that he had no patience for the endless meetings and Congressional voting rules, which required nine states to be in agreement before anything at all could be done. This situation created

Back of the State House, Philadelphia, 1799, by William Russell Birch.

gridlock by allowing a small minority of states to prevent any measure or action. He was further frustrated when his ideas were not met with enthusiasm, and in fact, when others didn't even think there *were* problems. Thomas Jefferson was not then a member of Congress, so he was not present, but he was extremely influential, not just over the Virginia delegates but also over much of the assembly. To Hamilton's deep annoyance, Jefferson believed the solution to the nation's financial crisis was to get rid of the central government altogether and replace the Continental Congress with a *committee*. Jefferson believed it best for each state to solve its own financial issues.

Excitable and passionate, Hamilton tended to dominate discussions. When he thought something was wrongheaded, he said so, without worrying about who he offended. Sometimes he didn't even need to speak: His passions ran so high, a person could often tell, just by looking at him, what he was thinking. "On most occasions," said one of his contemporaries, "when animated with the subject on which he was engaged, you could see the very workings of his soul."

He spent a great deal of his time trying to convince the delegates from Rhode Island to approve an import duty for the entire country that would allow Congress to pay its war debts.

The Rhode Island delegates resisted because they felt their highly commercialized state would be hit particularly hard by such a duty. He had a difficult time with the Rhode Island matter partly because so many delegates failed entirely to show up in Philadelphia, preferring to remain at home and take care of their estates, or their clients. Some divided their time between Congress and their roles in state governments, which many considered more important.

Then came a crisis: The officers in the Continental Army grew tired of not being paid and decided to do something about it. In what came to be known as the Newburgh Conspiracy, a group of officers hatched an outrageous plot to oust George Washington, march on Congress, take the members captive, and hold them hostage until the soldiers and officers received their pay.

Hamilton was in complete sympathy with the officers. He felt it was shameful that the government let soldiers go unfed, unclothed, and unpaid. He wrote to George Washington, offering the brash advice that Washington should use the officers' unrest to force Congress to act. Fortunately, Washington understood that the government must be in control of the military, not the other way around. He gently warned Hamilton of the dangers of stirring anger in army officers for political purposes. "The army," Washington told Hamilton, was "a dangerous instrument to play with."

Washington's plan, instead, was to attend an officers' meeting in Newburgh, New York, where the Continental Army was encamped, with the goal of preventing "a civil horror from which there might be no receding." He entered the meeting, startling the officers, who hadn't expected him. He implored them to place their full confidence in him, promising to plead their case before Congress. He offered to read a letter from a Virginia congressman. He reached into his pocket for his spectacles, remarking offhand that he'd "not only grown gray but almost blind" in the service of his country. His audience was deeply moved. In the words of Major Samuel Shaw, an officer in an artillery regiment, the natural genuineness and sincerity of Washington's appeal were far more effective than a high-flown speech. Mention of his growing nearsightedness "forced its way to the heart" and "moistened every eye." As a result, the officers set aside their conspiracy and put their trust in Washington. In the words of one historian, that was the day George Washington's spectacles saved the republic.

The threatened mutiny scared Congress into appointing a committee to address the problem. Hamilton chaired the committee, urging the others to adopt a measure to give officers some compensation. What happened next deeply distressed Hamilton: He was accused of fermenting the rebellion so that he could force a strong central government on the people.

Frustrated, he recognized that he would not be able to bring about the structural changes he felt the country so desperately needed. On May 14, 1783, he wrote to Governor Clinton of New York, expressing his wish to be replaced so he could return to private life. "Having no future view in public life," he wrote, "I owe it to myself without delay to enter upon the care of my private concerns in earnest."

As Hamilton waited to be relieved from his duties, Congress received word that a fresh mutiny had erupted. Eighty soldiers in the Pennsylvania militia in Lancaster broke away from their officers and were marching to Philadelphia to demand the back pay they were owed. When the insurgents reached Philadelphia on Friday, June 20, their ranks had swelled to several hundred. They surrounded the Pennsylvania State House and poked their bayonets into the windows of the council chamber.

Members of Congress sat for three hours, harassed and besieged, listening as the angry soldiers called them out by name. At nightfall, the delegates left the building unharmed and assembled in the home of Elias Boudinot, one of the first friends

Hamilton made upon his arrival in North America. That evening, Hamilton drafted a resolution, which Congress adopted, stating that if Pennsylvania did not rein in the militia, Congress would relocate to New Jersey. When the state of Pennsylvania failed to call off the soldiers, Congress fled to New Jersey and set up offices in Princeton.

6

Capitalism: A New Vision for America

'Tis by introducing order into our finances—
by restoring public credit—not by gaining battles,
that we are finally to gain our object.

— Alexander Hamilton

While encamped in Princeton with Congress and waiting to be relieved from his position, Hamilton tried once more. He drafted a resolution calling for a convention to revise the Articles of Confederation, listing the defects he believed were glaringly obvious. He offered what he considered a more workable plan. Following philosopher John Locke's notion that a legitimate government requires checks and balances and separate powers, his plan included a three-part government. He showed his plan to James Madison and a few others, but they were skeptical that the idea would work, and Hamilton was unable to muster enough support.

The problem was that Hamilton's ideas for the new nation were contrary to the vision held by a group of influential Americans led by Thomas Jefferson.

Outwardly Jefferson and Hamilton were as different as could be. Jefferson was cool and impassive, whereas Hamilton was moody, talkative, and emotional. Jefferson was born into the luxury of a Virginian plantation. Because his father, a self-made man, worked his way into the class of landed gentlemen, he was the Virginian equivalent of an aristocrat. His mother was also born into wealth. Jefferson was educated in a preparatory school and the College of William & Mary. Like Hamilton, he was a brilliant student, quickly outpacing his classmates. At the age of twenty-five, he inherited five thousand acres and numerous slaves, but—also like Hamilton—he was driven by ambition. Wanting to be more than a wealthy planter, he became a lawyer as a step toward a career of public service.

While Hamilton imagined an urbanized and capitalistic nation, Jefferson envisioned a pastoral America of small towns, where governments were local, states would control their own destiny, and the federal government would remain small and weak. For Jefferson, the ideal society was one in which workers owned their own farms. "Those who labor in the earth are the chosen people of God," he said. In his view, farm ownership offered independence and dignity, even if the farm did no more than provide sustenance for the family.

Jefferson believed that land was the source of all wealth and that the most useful—and hence important—class of citizens were farmers and planters. He would have been happy for America to continue as a nation of farmers, exchanging raw goods for finished products. He disliked mercantilism and capitalism on the theory that they created an unquenchable thirst for money and material possessions.

Jefferson believed that a mercantile and manufacturing society was the lowest and most corrupt of cultures because it was structured around money. He compared industrialized cities to sores on a human body.

Jefferson's views about money had deep roots in European history. Early Americans, who took Bible study seriously, were familiar with such verses as "The love of money is the root of all evil." Christians had long regarded charging interest on loans as sinful. This view came from seeing money as fixed, like land, where the only way to get more was to take someone else's.

Hamilton, who grasped the principles of mercantilism, understood that through investments, lending, and borrowing, it was possible to enlarge the size of the pie, allowing everyone to have a larger share. A person could start with nothing at all, borrow money to start a business, and then pay back the loan with interest. It was a situation that rewarded everyone: the lender, the borrower, and the consumer, who now had more options.

What Hamilton saw as chaos—states imposing their own tariffs and border patrols, essentially fleecing one another—Jefferson viewed as mostly a good thing. As Jefferson saw it, the individual states were in the process of establishing themselves as sovereign mini-nations. He believed that the problems then facing the new nation were "so light in comparison with those existing in every other government on Earth, that our citizens may certainly be considered as in the happiest political situation that exists."

For Jefferson, Hamilton's desire for a centralized government taking power from the states meant loss of individual freedom and liberty. In fact, for Jefferson, the entire reason the Revolutionary War had been fought was to free local governments from the tyranny of a foreign government that collected taxes and laid down rules—and in Jefferson's view, everything outside of Virginia was foreign.

What mattered to Jefferson was individual liberty. The irony, of which Jefferson was well aware, was that his idea of liberty included the freedom to hold slaves. He struggled with the evils

inherent in slavery, saying at times such things as, "There is nothing I would not sacrifice to a practicable plan of abolishing every
vestige of this moral and political depravity." The operative word
for Jefferson, though, was "practicable." Because he didn't believe
whites and blacks could live together as equals, he didn't see a
practical way to end slavery. He justified slavery by comparing
those enslaved to the laborers in a mercantile society and arguing
that slaves were better off because their masters kept them fed
and clothed and provided for. He acknowledged that slaves were
subject to "bodily coercion," but argued that lowly workers in an
industrialized society were even more victimized.

Jefferson understood that Hamilton's vision for America—
central rule and a capitalistic economy—threatened the agrarian
way of life. Despite his misgivings about slavery, he insisted that
if Virginia wanted to remain a slave state, nobody had the right to
tell Virginia it couldn't or insist on a new constitution that took
away Virginia's right to self-governance.

In the face of so much resistance, Hamilton had to accept
defeat. On the back of his plan for a three-part federal government, he scribbled the woeful comment: "Plan for a government, presented at Princeton, but abandoned for lack of support." He returned home to his family in Albany, disillusioned

and completely demoralized, remarking in a letter to John Jay:

Our prospects are not flattering. Every day proves the inefficacy of the present confederation ... It is to be hoped that when prejudice and folly have run themselves out of breath, we may return to reason and correct our errors.

On September 3, 1783, the Treaty of Paris officially ended the Revolutionary War. Soon after, in November, the British army evacuated New York City. Sullen, the army troops marched one last time through the cobblestoned streets to the harbor, where vessels of the Royal Navy awaited them. Citizens heard the clattering of horses and rattling of heavy artillery, and looked out their windows, but the streets were largely empty. It was a solemn moment.

Shortly afterward, George Washington triumphantly led the Continental Army into Manhattan to reclaim the city.

Washington's Entry into New York on the Evacuation of the City by the British in 1783, c. 1857, Currier & Ives.

With the war over, the Americans were left to govern themselves, undertaking what has been called "the great American experiment," defined this way: With a full understanding of human imperfections and the tendency for those in power to abuse it, could common people govern themselves?

Hamilton, Eliza, and baby Philip rented a house in the city at 57 Wall Street. Their neighborhood was a mix of modest homes, shops, and offices. When the windows were open, the Hamiltons could hear merchants hawking their wares, the clopping of horse hooves, the tingling of cowbells, and the rumbling of carts. Hamilton established his law practice, which he operated out of his home. Already famous for his intellect and his principles—and married into one of the most prominent families in the state—he had no trouble attracting clients.

Hamilton may have been a genius at understanding the complexities of international banking and commerce, but either he was terrible with his personal finances, or he didn't care about acquiring his own wealth. When he set up his law practice, his fees were low, and he frequently worked without pay when he felt that someone too poor to hire a lawyer had suffered an injustice. He also passed up the opportunity to buy prime Manhattan real estate at dirt-cheap prices.

7

Due Process of Law

*The voice of the people has been said to be
the voice of God; and, however generally this maxim
has been quoted and believed, it is not true to fact.
The people are turbulent and changing; they
seldom judge or determine right.*

— Alexander Hamilton

ew York was a city divided. Prior to the war, large numbers of New Yorkers were Loyalists and British sympathizers. About a third of the city's residents, many of them members of the elite and merchant class, were sorry to see the British go. Some of the reasons were practical. There had been advantages to being part of an empire. The Royal Navy no longer guaranteed the safety of American ships at sea, so American farmers were having difficulty selling their crops and products in foreign markets. English banks no longer provided badly needed credit.

Patriots and the returning soldiers were deeply resentful of the devastation the British had wreaked on their city and the brutalities committed against Patriots who had remained in the city during the occupation. The British had imprisoned thousands of captured American soldiers on ships, where many perished during the freezing winters, and allowed Loyalists to ransack Patriot homes and businesses. Fires destroyed entire sections of the city.

Fights broke out in the streets as returning soldiers demanded their homes and property back. Articles appeared in the Patriot newspapers calling for all Loyalists who had remained in the city during the occupation to leave voluntarily or risk being exiled—a call that Hamilton recognized as absurd. How could anyone be sure who had been sympathetic to the British and who had not? There were plenty of Patriots, including his good friend Hercules Mulligan, who had remained in the city to spy on the British and send reports back to the Patriots. Such spies were, to all outward appearances, British sympathizers.

Hamilton felt that the eyes of the world were on them. Would the American experiment succeed, or would the new country make a mess of it? To Hamilton, it looked as if they were about to botch everything, forgetting the very precepts of liberty they had fought for. Hamilton was therefore horrified when New York governor George Clinton "condemned, imprisoned, and punished the Loyalists most unmercifully." In the words of one contemporary, the Loyalists "were by [Clinton's] orders tarred and feathered, carted, whipped, fined, and banished, and in short, every kind of cruelty."

The legislature of New York, under enormous public pressure to punish the Loyalists, passed three anti-Loyalist laws. The Trespass Act enabled returning Patriots to sue Loyalists who had occupied their property during their absence. The Citation Act said that anyone owing a debt to a Loyalist didn't have to pay it back. The Confiscation Act prevented Loyalists from reclaiming their own property that had been confiscated during the war.

Hamilton spoke out against all three laws, publishing a letter urging citizens not to give in to "furious and dark passions," imploring them instead to embrace the generous and humane values that inspired the fight for freedom. He argued that revenge violated national honor. He shocked many by suggesting that the anti-Loyalist laws were motivated by greedy people who wanted to get rich through plunder in a clear violation of due process of law.

DUE PROCESS refers to the rights of citizens to receive fair treatment under the law and through the courts.

The concept of due process in English law goes all the way back to the year 1215, when King John of England, to prevent a rebellion, signed the Magna Carta, or Great Charter, which gave rights to certain groups of citizens. The Magna Carta was the first written constitution in European history. Many of its provisions benefitted only the ruling classes, and the majority of people in England had no voice in their government. Still, the Magna Carta established

Because Hamilton denounced the anti-Loyalist laws, and because he looked to the Bank of England as a model for the kind of bank America should create, people concluded that he must secretly be a Loyalist and hence an enemy of the new republic. What he did next irked his critics even more: He accepted Loyalists as his clients, defending them from charges brought against them by the returning Patriots. His most famous and important anti-Loyalist case came to be called *Rutgers v. Waddington*.

certain principles of liberty and freedom, including the guarantee that no "free man" could be imprisoned or deprived of property except by the lawful judgment of his peers or by the law of the land, a concept that came to be called due process of law. Due process became part of English common law—meaning part of the culture and custom of the people, respected by judges and courts. English common law came to include such practices as trial by jury.

English common law was adopted by American colonial courts. New York's first constitution, like other state constitutions, largely adopted English common law.

Elizabeth Rutgers was a widow and a Patriot who fled the city when the British invaded, leaving behind a brew house and malt house. While she was gone, equipment was stolen from her property. In September 1778, a British general assigned her property to two British merchants, Benjamin Waddington and Evelyn Pierrepont, who in turn appointed Joshua Waddington, Benjamin's nephew, as the brewery supervisor. All three spent a great deal of money replacing the missing equipment and restoring the property. They used the rebuilt property rent-free until May 1, 1780, during which time they earned enormous profits. When the war ended, Benjamin Waddington and Evelyn Pierrepont returned to England, taking the profits with them. Joshua Waddington remained in New York. On November 23, 1783, two days before the British evacuated New York, a fire destroyed the brewery.

Upon her return, Elizabeth Rutgers sued Joshua Waddington under the Trespass Act for 8,000 pounds in back rent for the time he used her property. Hamilton accepted Joshua Waddington as his client.

The plight of Elizabeth Rutgers—a widow in her seventies—aroused public sympathy. As the aunt of New York's attorney general, she was also well connected. It was a dream case for Rutgers's lawyers. Given the public outrage on behalf of Elizabeth Rutgers, Joshua Waddington was among the most hated people in New York. Rutgers's lawyers claimed that the anti-Loyalist laws did not violate due process because they offered justice to those who had been plundered. Public opinion was firmly on Rutgers's side.

Hamilton believed Waddington had a strong defense. Unlike many of the Loyalists who had simply used or even devalued the property of Patriots in their absence, Rutgers's property had been in shambles when Waddington stepped in, and at his own expense, he'd restored the value. Hamilton's chief defense was that anti-Loyalist laws violated the peace treaty signed by the United States and England because the treaty decreed that neither side would take further steps of retaliation. What were the anti-Loyalist laws if not retaliation?

Public attention was riveted on Joshua Waddington's trial, held in the New York City Mayor's Court. Rutgers's lawyers rebutted Hamilton's argument that New York was bound by the peace treaty by pointing out that the Articles of Confederation expressly reserved to the states their "freedom, sovereignty, and independence." In other words, Rutgers's lawyers argued that a treaty signed by the United States was not binding on New York— an argument that left Hamilton aghast. How could the federal government have any authority or credibility with other nations if states considered themselves unbound by federal treaties?

Hamilton also argued that the anti-Loyalist laws violated international rules of warfare, which permitted an occupying army to use property in the enemy territory. Owners of occupied property were not entitled to compensation unless allowed for in the peace treaty.

Finally, Hamilton argued that the law violated the New York Constitution, which guaranteed basic rights—including the right to due process of law—to *all* citizens. Rutgers's lawyers conceded that the New York Constitution included the right to due process, but claimed that a statute could overrule the constitution because the statute was more democratic in that it was passed by lawmakers selected by the people. The New York Constitution, on the other hand, had been adopted by an ad hoc committee.

Thus, essentially, the case was about which legal authority was higher: the national government or the states? A constitution or a statute? International laws of warfare or a New York law?

For Hamilton, the case was also about the limits of democracy: Should the majority be allowed to enact any laws they wanted? For Hamilton, the answer was a resounding *no*. Without limits on what lawmakers could do, there was nothing to stop the majority from passing laws that brutalized the minority—a concept John Adams later called the tyranny of the majority. Hamilton was also afraid of too much democracy, which in his view could lead to anarchy—a total absence of government, law, and order. Remembering the mob violence against the Loyalists prior to the war and the soldiers' threats of mutiny afterward, he understood how easy it would be for demagogues to grab power by inciting and stoking mob anger.

A DEMAGOGUE is a leader who comes to power by making false claims and promises, and by appealing to darker emotions like prejudice and fear.

Hamilton's fears of demagoguery had deep roots in western philosophy. Plato, an ancient Greek philosopher, often considered one of the greatest and most influential philosophers of all time, disliked democracy because he feared people were too often guided by unreliable emotions instead of careful analysis, and thus easily led into wars and destructive behavior. Plato believed, essentially, that the problem with democracy was that anyone able to con a large enough group of people could become the ruler, a situation that encouraged and rewarded demagoguery.

The court's ruling in *Rutgers v. Waddington* disappointed everyone. The court essentially ducked the important issues by offering a compromise. The court backed away from striking down the anti-Loyalist laws but awarded Mrs. Rutgers only 800 pounds instead of 8,000, refusing to allow her to collect rent from Waddington during the time he used the property with permission of the British. Even a partial victory for Hamilton was stunning given the intensity of public hatred of Joshua Waddington.

For a lawyer willing to defend the Loyalists, there was no shortage of work. In Hamilton's words, "Legislative folly has afforded so plentiful a harvest to us lawyers that we have scarcely a moment to spare from the substantial business of reaping." During a three-year period, he defended forty-five individuals prosecuted under the Trespass Act, and twenty under the Confiscation and Citation Acts. He saw himself as a defender of due process. His enemies saw him as greedily accepting money to help scoundrels and thieves.

✶ ✶ ✶ ✶ ✶ ✶ ✶ ✶ ✶ ✶ ✶ ✶ ✶ ✶ ✶

Hamilton no doubt first met Aaron Burr, a native of New Jersey, before the war, but in 1783 in New York, for the first time, they moved in the same social circles and saw each other regularly, and even worked together on

Aaron Burr, c. 1800, attributed to Gilbert Stuart.

occasion. Both Hamilton and Burr were lawyers interested in politics, but their personalities were markedly different. Burr was secretive and reserved while Hamilton was outspoken to a fault. They were never close friends, and often opponents in the courtroom, but there was no hint of the hatred that would later bring them to the dueling ground in Weehawken.

Their lives, until then, had been curiously parallel. They were about the same age; Hamilton was one year older. Both lost their parents at an early age, although Burr, from a family of scholars and religious clerics, was taken in by wealthy relatives when both his parents died of smallpox. Both had unhappy childhoods. Burr, described as stubborn and mischievous, had often been beaten and felt alone.

Both were hailed as brilliant students. Burr entered Princeton at the age of thirteen and graduated three years later with highest honors. Both were considered dashingly handsome. In June 1776, while Hamilton was leading his artillery company, Burr joined George Washington's staff. By that point—before Washington became aware of Hamilton—Burr was already a war hero, having served valiantly in one of the first battles of the Revolutionary War, the Battle of Quebec.

Burr did not last long on Washington's staff. The reason

Burr quit isn't clear. Presumably he and Washington didn't get along. Burr served out the war under other generals. He harbored a secret jealousy, however, of those in Washington's inner circle, believing that Washington preferred men less qualified than himself.

When John Jay founded the Society for Promoting the Manumission of Slaves in New York, both Burr and Hamilton joined. The society was formed on the idea that *all* people were entitled to due process, and it began by protesting the horrifying practice of kidnapping black New Yorkers, both free and enslaved, and selling them as slaves elsewhere. The society, though, didn't go as far as Hamilton believed it should. For example, other members rejected his resolution that anyone who wanted to be a member had to free their own slaves. The society did, however, found the New York African Free School and raised funds for teachers' salaries and supplies, based on the understanding that education was vital for enabling freed blacks to participate fully in state politics and culture. Later the society lobbied the state legislature to put an end to the slave trade in New York, "a commerce so repugnant to humanity, and so inconsistent with the liberality and justice which should distinguish a free and enlightened people."

8

Steps in the Right Direction

*Most commercial nations have found it necessary
to institute banks and they have proved to be the happiest
engines that ever were invented for advancing trade.*

— Alexander Hamilton

n 1784, there wasn't a single bank in New York City. In fact,
there was only one financial institution in all the states.
The Bank of North America in Philadelphia was founded
by Robert Morris in 1781, modeled on the Bank of England.
While there was only one financial bank in the new nation,
there were numerous land banks, whose chief function was to lend
money to landowners against the value of their land. A financial
bank, in contrast, accepts cash deposits from individuals and
businesses, which it then lends to others.

Several directors of the Bank of North America wanted to open a bank in New York, so they turned to Hamilton for assistance. New York, still devastated from the British occupation and debt-ridden, lacked the resources to pull itself out of poverty. So Hamilton jumped at the chance to help New York acquire its own bank, seeing it as a way to help New York merchants get back on their feet.

Hamilton tried to get New York's bank chartered by the state, which would have made it part of the government, but there was too much resistance. Many in the rural parts of New York preferred a land bank, believing that a financial bank would benefit only merchants. The bigger problem was that many people viewed the entire practice of lending at interest as a dark art steeped in evil.

View of the Northeast Corner of Wall and William Streets, New York City, 1798, by Archibald Robertson. The Bank of New York can be seen at far right.

Steps in the Right Direction

Because he could not persuade the state to charter the bank, the Bank of New York opened its doors in 1784 as a private financial institution. The new bank was housed in the Walton Mansion, a three-story yellow-brick building on a street now known as Pearl Street. Hamilton wrote up papers incorporating the bank. He was voted one of the founding directors, but he remained a director for only a few years. He and John Jay both opened accounts and deposited money, but Hamilton never profited as a bank officer, perhaps because, always sensitive to criticism, he was afraid that his opponents would accuse him of greed.

THE BANK OF NEW YORK is still in existence today. In 2007, it merged with the Mellon Financial Corporation under a new name—the Bank of New York Mellon. Today the corporate offices of New York Mellon are housed in a skyscraper in the financial district at 225 Liberty Street. The bank boasts of being the nation's oldest financial institution—and of being founded by Alexander Hamilton himself.

The nation's financial situation continued deteriorating. Maryland and Virginia were in a heated dispute over use of the Potomac River and the Chesapeake Bay. In a move seen by others as greedy, New York taxed all goods entering from the West Indies, even though many of the goods were destined for other states. James Madison wrote to Thomas Jefferson to complain about the "present anarchy of our commerce." John Jay felt more apprehension for America's future than he had during the war. Even Washington came to doubt whether the American people were fit for self-governance. On May 18, 1786, he said, "That it is necessary to revise and amend the Articles of Confederation, I entertain *no* doubt . . . Something must be done, or the fabric must fall, for it certainly is tottering."

After resolving their water dispute, Maryland and Virginia invited the other states to participate in a convention in Annapolis to decide how to regulate trade and reduce the constant bickering between the states. It wasn't quite what Hamilton wanted— he wanted to scrap the Articles of Confederation altogether and write a whole new constitution—but he saw the convention in Annapolis as a necessary first step. He wanted to be the delegate from New York, but Governor Clinton didn't want to send him. Clinton, adamantly opposed to the idea of a strong central government, viewed Hamilton as a political enemy. He wanted to send someone who would fight to maintain state sovereignty. But Hamilton had recently run for state assembly—and won, mostly because of his popularity among the city's business owners and because he had the support of the Schuylers and their connections. During his run for assembly, he learned how to play politics, organizing and rallying his supporters. His friends and allies got behind him and made sure he was appointed as New York's delegate to the convention in Annapolis.

On September 2, 1786, he said good-bye to his family, mounted his horse, and headed toward Annapolis. He fell ill during the first part of the journey, so he stopped in Philadelphia to regain his strength. He arrived in Maryland on September 9. He and the other delegates lodged at George Mann's City Tavern, an elegant three-story brick hostelry large enough to sleep a hundred people. Only twelve delegates representing five states—New Jersey, New York, Pennsylvania, Delaware, and Virginia—were present. On the bright side, the delegates who showed up were strong critics of the Articles of Confederation, so there were no angry debates.

They named themselves the Commissioners to Remedy Defects of the Federal Government. The delegates agreed that a little tinkering wouldn't do. To resolve the disputes between the states and fix the financial crisis, the Articles of Confederation would have to be thoroughly rewritten—something that couldn't happen with only five states represented. Hamilton drafted a resolution calling for a special convention in Philadelphia to revise the Articles. He showed his first draft to James Madison, who represented Virginia. Madison found the language so scorching and inflammatory that he advised Hamilton to tone it down or "all Virginia will be against you." Hamilton followed his advice. He presented a more diplomatic version to the other delegates, who unanimously adopted the resolution.

At the same time the Commissioners to Remedy Defects of the Federal Government were signing their resolution, violence erupted in Massachusetts. The state of Massachusetts tried to pay its war debt by imposing a steep tax on the farmers. Four thousand farmers rebelled, grabbing pitchforks and descending on courthouses in what came to be called Shays' Rebellion. The rebellion dragged on for months, beginning with the rebels' attempt to capture the federal arsenal in Springfield, Massachusetts, and continuing with several skirmishes throughout the winter between the insurgents and the state militia.

The rebellion shocked the nation. Hamilton and others linked the rebellion to eight years of war, which for so many citizen-soldiers glorified and normalized violent protests against rulers. George Washington was horrified by the rebellion. Even Samuel Adams, a champion of revolutions, condemned the rebels.

Thomas Jefferson, in contrast, had a nonchalant attitude toward the rebellion. He wrote, "I hold it that a little rebellion now and then is a good thing, and as necessary in the political world as storms in the physical" and "a medicine necessary for the sound health of government." He insisted that rebellions were good because they prevented governments from encroaching too much on individual liberty. Thomas Jefferson was in the minority, though. The public was ready for stability.

The timing of the rebellion played perfectly into the hands of the Commissioners to Remedy Defects of the Federal Government. Copies of their resolution circulated along with news of the rebellion. Soon Pennsylvania, North Carolina, Virginia, and New Jersey agreed to send delegates to Philadelphia to rewrite the Articles. By the time the rebels in Massachusetts surrendered, the Continental Congress itself called upon all states to send delegates to Philadelphia to amend the Articles, even though doing so could mean signing its own death warrant.

9

The Good Ship Hamilton

Why has government been instituted at all?
Because the passions of men will not conform to the
dictates of reason and justice without constraint.

— Alexander Hamilton

eorge Clinton railed against Hamilton for advocating a consolidation of the states, but there was nothing he could do to prevent Hamilton from being named a New York delegate to Philadelphia. Instead, Clinton outmaneuvered him. Under the voting rules, New York would have one vote, so Clinton silenced Hamilton by making sure two other delegates would be sent from New York. The other two, Robert Yates and John Lansing, were friends of Clinton's and entirely shared his views, so there would always be two votes against one.

On a mild day in May 1787, Hamilton arrived in Philadelphia. He stayed at the Indian Queen Tavern, the city's largest boarding house, located on Third between Chestnut and Market Streets, a charming, tree-lined street not far from Independence Hall.

On May 18, 1787, the first day of the proceedings dawned gray and overcast. Rain was falling as the delegates entered Independence Hall and took their seats in the spacious room. With the shutters pulled tight to keep out insects and prying eyes, the room was dim and sweltering. Twelve of the thirteen states were represented. Only Rhode Island, nicknamed Rogue Island, boycotted the convention. George Washington was named the presiding officer and took his place in a high-backed chair at the head of the room. Washington knew, as did everyone else, that he'd be the overwhelming choice to lead the country when a new government was formed. Afraid of appearing to grab power, he mostly remained silent.

For the entire first month, Hamilton said nothing at all. He had no voice in setting up the rules and voting procedures because anything he wanted was immediately overruled by Lansing and Yates. He grew listless and depressed, listening to the debates and suggestions. The delegates divided into the Federalists, like Hamilton and James Madison, who were in favor of a strong central government, and the Anti-Federalists, like Lansing and Yates, who argued that no single government had ever ruled so vast an area with such diversity of commerce and peoples. They believed it impossible. The Anti-Federalists greatly outnumbered the others. Most delegates, in fact, when introducing themselves, explained outright that they had orders from their state governments to do all they could to protect state sovereignty.

The delegates from New Jersey submitted a plan that was little more than an amendment to the Articles. They suggested giving the federal government power to regulate commerce between the states while keeping all other matters almost entirely as they were. James Madison, on behalf of Virginia, proposed what Hamilton considered a better plan: two houses of Congress and an executive branch, whose head, the president, would serve a single term. The problem for Hamilton was that the members of the executive branch and the judges would all be selected by the state representatives and would have limited terms, which in his view gave too much power to the individual states at the expense of a stable central government.

On June 18, Hamilton broke his silence and took the floor, talking nonstop for five hours—a stunning length of time but by no means a record. One delegate from New Jersey had held the floor for two solid days, talking about states' rights. Hamilton opened his speech with a warning that his views were radical and might startle some people. Then he gave his suggestions. He thought federal laws should supersede state laws on all occasions. He wanted state governors to be appointed by the federal government. He argued that the federal government should be able to veto any state laws. He wanted federal judges appointed for life so that they would be above politics and able to protect the rights of those in the minority.

Then, he went even further and suggested that states were altogether unnecessary and should be abolished. If there were no separate states at all, he explained, the economy would be much stronger, and a national army would never again be left to starve. He wanted the senators and president elected by popular vote to serve lifetime tenures, with exceptions for bad behavior. Unfortunately, though he carefully used the word "republic" to describe the new nation—meaning that no powers were to be hereditary—he used the words "elective monarch" to describe the president.

When he finished speaking, there was polite applause. Later this speech was used against him by his enemies to paint him as a monarchist. In fact, immediately after Hamilton's speech, Yates and Lansing wrote to Clinton, denouncing the entire convention as a wicked conspiracy to install a monarchy. At the time, though, Hamilton's suggestions caused very little stir. While the majority of his countrymen believed power should reside in the states, Hamilton wasn't the only delegate who believed radical changes were needed to bring about stability.

Some even praised his speech, including William Samuel Johnson and Gouverneur Morris, both of whom who later signed the Constitution.

It was clear from the debates that followed that Hamilton's idea of lifetime tenure for senators would not be approved, so he joined Madison in arguing for the longest possible terms. The group appealed to the smaller states by proposing that each state elect two senators, which would assure the small states considerable power.

Then, abruptly, Hamilton left Philadelphia and returned to New York, saying only that he was being called away for a few days on private business. George Mason, a Virginia delegate, told Thomas Jefferson in a letter that Hamilton went home frustrated and humiliated because Yates and Lansing, in every instance, voted against him.

Back in New York, Hamilton plunged back into his law

practice and spent time with his family. He and Eliza now had three children: Philip, age five; Angelica, age four; and their third child, Alexander Jr., just over a year old. They also took in and raised a girl named Fanny, who was left an orphan when her mother, a Revolutionary War widow, died. The family belonged to an Episcopal parish church. Eliza read to the children from the Bible each morning before breakfast.

A few weeks after returning home, Hamilton received a letter from George Washington. "I am sorry you went away—I wish you were back," Washington wrote. He went on to explain that the deadlock was alarming; he was in despair and no longer hoped for a good result. He said, "The men who oppose a strong and energetic government are, in my opinion, narrow minded politicians, or are under the influence of local views."

Not long afterward, in mid-July, Hamilton learned that Lansing and Yates had returned to New York in a huff because they didn't like the direction the conference was heading, which Hamilton took as a good sign. He didn't return to Philadelphia, though. Under the rules, a state had to have more than one delegate present in order to vote, so if he went back to the conference, he would still be in the frustrating position of having no real voice in the proceedings. In fact, as he later learned, things *were* moving in the direction he wanted. The delegates agreed that the president should be elected by a nationwide vote so that he could stand up to abuses of power by Congress. The delegates also agreed to divide power between states and the federal government, with states controlling such institutions as schools and police departments. Supreme Court justices were to be appointed for life by the president, with "advice and consent" of the Senate.

Hamilton returned to Philadelphia at the end of the summer. By then, most of the work was done. While the final document fell short of what Hamilton wanted, it contained a number of things he'd worked hard for, most importantly a powerful federal government. Also, some delegates had wanted to deny foreign-born individuals the right to run for national office, something Hamilton was against. An immigrant himself, he felt America would be stronger if it was welcoming to foreigners. The final document required only the president to be a natural-born citizen.

The Constitution also included compromises and omissions that would haunt America for generations to come. Because each state's number of representatives in the House would be proportional to its population, a dispute arose about how to count slaves. The men, women, and children enslaved at the time were considered property. The South, which had a large slave population, wanted the slaves counted as humans and not property so southern states would have enough power in Congress to prevent the North from outlawing slavery. The North didn't want the enslaved to count because if they did, the southern states would likely control the House of Representatives. So in a strange twist, southern slave owners wanted their slaves counted as humans instead of property so that they could have the votes necessary to ensure that the enslaved remained property. The compromise was that each slave counted as three-fifths of a person, a number that gave the South more power than if slaves didn't count at all, but still kept them short of a majority. Later Hamilton explained that without this compromise, the union would have never been formed.

Another controversy erupted over whether to ban the importing of new slaves. Georgia and the Carolinas threatened to walk out if importing slaves was banned. Eventually they compromised, giving Congress authority to forbid importing slaves, but not before 1808.

The Constitution never addressed the question of whether the states joined the union by contract, which would allow them to secede if they chose, or whether the states, in signing, gave up the power to leave the union. In effect, the framers of the

Constitution compromised or simply left out the most contro-versial points, kicking down the road questions about slavery and the limits of federal power.

On September 17, 1787, Hamilton signed the Constitution along with thirty-eight other delegates from twelve states—with Rhode Island still absent. The next task was to get the Constitu-tion ratified. One of the ground rules decided by the convention was that the Constitution would not go into effect until at least nine states ratified it. So Hamilton returned to New York with a major task: persuade the New York legislature to approve the new Constitution.

★ ★ ★ ★ ★ ★ ★ ★ ★ ★ ★ ★ ★ ★ ★

Clinton and his allies launched a campaign against Hamil-ton and the Constitution. They continued to accuse him of being a monarchist interested in establishing banks to enrich himself and his friends, and to ingratiate himself with wealthy merchants. They also accused him of maneuvering for a posi-tion in the federal government and engineering a powerful federal

Scene at Signing of the Constitution of the United States, c. 1960, by Howard Chandler Christy. This painting hangs in the United States House of Representatives.

government as part of a personal power grab. They sought to discredit him by spreading the rumor that he had wormed his way into George Washington's inner circle but that Washington had contemptuously rejected him.

Hamilton, stung, wrote to Washington asking him to denounce the accusations as false. Washington complied. Hamilton then fought back with his pen. Hoping that rational arguments would sway public opinion, he launched a series of essays, known today as the *Federalist Papers*, to explain the new Constitution and sell it to a skeptical public. He and Eliza were sailing upriver on the Hudson, on their way to visit Albany, when he wrote the first essay and outlined the entire project. He opened the series by noting that Americans were about to decide the fate of the union and answer the question of whether common people were capable of governing themselves. The initial

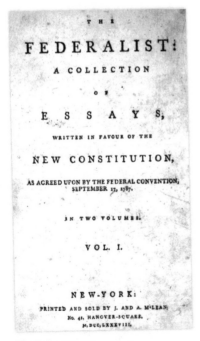

The *Federalist*, title page.

plan was a modest one—about twenty essays in all. He recruited John Jay and James Madison to work with him. By the time the project was finished, Hamilton, Jay, and Madison had written eighty-five essays. John Jay wrote five, and James Madison wrote twenty-nine. Hamilton wrote a staggering fifty-one.

Back in New York City, Hamilton labored for eight months, writing roughly two essays per week at three-day intervals and publishing them in four of the five New York newspapers. The deadlines were so tight that as the printer was setting the type for one essay, Hamilton was already furiously writing the next. Initially the three authors showed one another drafts, but after a while, the tight deadlines made it impossible. Hamilton was still practicing law, so he squeezed in the writing around meetings with clients and court appearances.

He worked with the intensity of a man possessed. His writing routine was to think for a while about his topic, then "retire to sleep without regard to the hour of the night and having slept six or seven hours, he rose and having taken strong coffee, seated himself at his table, where he would remain six, seven, or eight hours. And the product of his rapid pen required little correction for the press."

He fully recognized the limits and imperfections of the

Constitution but defended it anyway, believing it far superior to the Articles of Confederation and capable of creating a workable government. "I never expect to see a perfect work from an imperfect man," he explained. Mostly, though, he was pleased with the new Constitution. He wanted a government to be "by the people," not because he trusted the people, but because he trusted state legislatures even less. During the course of writing, the essays evolved from a passionate defense of the new Constitution into an extended treatise on government and human nature.

✦ ✦ ✦ ✦ ✦ ✦ ✦ ✦ ✦ ✦ ✦ ✦ ✦ ✦ ✦

A preliminary vote in New York showed that Hamilton faced an uphill battle. Most delegates at the meeting, called the state convention, were adamantly opposed to the new Constitution. New York was divided by region, with each region sending delegates to the convention. The rural areas—led by Clinton and his allies—mostly opposed the new Constitution. New York City was largely in favor. Hamilton's problem was that the rural parts of New York had more people, more delegates, and thus greater power in the state government.

In New York, the *Federalist Papers* did little to sway the population. In the words of one New Yorker, the essays were simply not intelligible to the common people. The *Federalist Papers* were, however, influential in Virginia because the word went around that Madison, one of Virginia's favorite sons, had a hand in them.

Hamilton's only hope for New York was for nine other states to ratify the Constitution before New York had the chance to vote, forming a union and leaving New Yorkers frightened by the prospect of becoming a small, weak state surrounded by a more powerful United States in an unequal power balance.

On December 7, 1787, Delaware became the first state to ratify the new Constitution. Four others followed in rapid succession: Pennsylvania, New Jersey, Georgia, and Connecticut. Four more were needed to form a union. Massachusetts balked because the Constitution lacked basic protections such as freedom of speech, religion, and the press. After being assured that a bill of rights would soon be added, Massachusetts, South Carolina, and Maryland ratified the Constitution.

Only one more state was needed. Virginia and New York held their conventions at the same time. Hamilton knew from correspondence with James Madison that Virginia was leaning toward ratification.

The New York convention was held in Poughkeepsie, New York, the state capital at the time and the heart of Clinton country. The convention itself was held in the Dutchess County Courthouse. Hamilton's plan was to stall the vote until Virginia voted.

As the delegates devised rules to govern the convention, Hamilton inserted the rule that before a vote could be taken, each provision of the Constitution would need to be discussed and debated. The effect was to turn the conference into a grueling marathon debate that dragged on for weeks. The lengthy discussion over each word and phrase allowed the tireless Hamilton, a master lawyer, to shine. In the words of James Kent, another New York lawyer present at the convention, "[T]he mighty mind of Hamilton would at times bear down all opposition by its comprehensive grasp and the strength of his reasoning powers." A newspaper described him as a "political porcupine, armed at all points." But Hamilton and his fellow Federalists were vastly outnumbered, and the opposition was fierce.

After several exhausting weeks, the conference was interrupted by showstopping news: New Hampshire had ratified the Constitution. Nine states had voted in favor, forming a union. The question remained whether the union would consist of nine states or more. Soon afterward, at noon on July 2, a messenger interrupted Governor Clinton, who was delivering a speech, with the news that Virginia, too, had ratified the Constitution. Only three states had not ratified: New York, North Carolina and Rhode Island. As Hamilton feared, Clinton vowed to hold out, even if New York stood alone as an independent republic.

Anti-Federalists then begin to insist on amendments to the Constitution and threatened to withdraw if their demands were not met. Hamilton proposed a face-saving measure: circulate a letter to the other states concerning the defects instead of ratifying with conditions.

When even this wasn't enough, Hamilton devised a shocking threat: If New York did not ratify the Constitution, New York City would secede from the state and join the union on its own, leaving the rural areas landlocked and isolated. The threat worked. Enough delegates switched their position. On July 26, 1788, New York ratified the Constitution by a very narrow margin. North Carolina did not ratify until 1789, and Rhode Island didn't join the union until May 29, 1790.

✳ ✳ ✳ ✳ ✳ ✳ ✳ ✳ ✳ ✳ ✳ ✳ ✳ ✳

New York City celebrated with a parade called the Grand Federal Procession, organized by the city's merchants. The centerpiece was a fully rigged model ship, twenty-seven

feet long and ten feet wide, pulled by ten white horses, honoring the hero of the hour, Alexander Hamilton. The ship, named the Federal Ship Hamilton, had billowing sails and a banner that proclaimed:

Behold the federal ship of fame
The Hamilton we call her name;
To every craft she gives employ;
Sure cartmen have their share of joy.

At eight on the morning of the parade, Hamilton and his family emerged from their home and gathered with neighbors to watch the parade. At ten o'clock, thirteen guns were fired from the Federal Ship Hamilton, signaling the start of the celebration. Horsemen with trumpets led the parade from the fields down Broadway to Great Dock Street, through Hanover Square, ending on Bullock Street at Bayard's Tavern. Following the horsemen was an artillery company and five thousand tradesmen: carpenters, furriers, florists, hatters, hairdressers, stonemasons, painters, and others. Lawyers and judges marched with the parade, joyfully waving copies of the new Constitution.

Federal Ship Hamilton, date and artist unknown.

The bakers carried a ten-pound "federal loaf." The butchers carried a banner—which depicted the heads of three bulls and a boar, plus two axes—proclaiming:

Skin me well, dress me neat,

And send me aboard the federal fleet.

It was the high point of Hamilton's political career. He was now a national figure and a local hero. He'd once believed that such respect and hero status could only be earned on the battlefield. Instead, his iconic status came through his pen and his intellect.

✦ ✦ ✦ ✦ ✦ ✦ ✦ ✦ ✦ ✦ ✦ ✦ ✦ ✦ ✦

The *Federalist Papers* stand today as some of the most important commentaries on the Constitution. When interpreting the Constitution, federal judges and the Supreme Court frequently turn to the *Federalist Papers* as an authority on how to read and understand the Constitution.

10

Secretary of the Treasury

*A national debt, if it is not excessive,
will be to us a national blessing.*

— *Alexander Hamilton*

obody was surprised on April 6, 1789, when George Washington was officially elected the first president. The election was expected to be a landslide, and it was. When Washington learned of the election results, he already had his bags packed. The new president journeyed from his Mount Vernon home to New York City, the temporary capital of the new nation. In each town he passed, citizens flocked to see him, throwing flower petals on the street, erecting triumphal arches, and ringing church bells.

ELECTIONS then, as now, were decided through the Electoral College, a complex system of delegates selected by the states: The states elected their delegates to the Electoral College, who then elected the president. The original idea behind the Electoral College was that uneducated masses could not be trusted with important decisions, and educated men must have the power to override a disastrous popular choice. Today, while nothing in the Constitution or federal law governs how electoral delegates vote, state laws and political parties generally require them to

On his way to New York, Washington stopped in Philadelphia at the home of Robert Morris, formerly the superintendent of finance for the Continental Congress who had once given Hamilton the job of tax collector for New York. In a private conversation, Washington asked Morris, "What are we to do with this heavy debt?" Morris, who for years had been on the receiving end of Hamilton's lengthy letters offering financial advice regarding the new nation, said, "There is but one man in the United States who can tell you; that is, Alexander Hamilton."

vote according to the popular vote in their state.

Prior to the ratification of the Twelfth Amendment in 1804, the Electoral College voted for the president, and whoever came in second place became the vice president. The problems this caused were apparent in the election of 1796, when the newly elected president and vice president, John Adams and Thomas Jefferson, were from different political parties. Today, as a result of the Twelfth Amendment, the president selects the vice president as a running mate and the the Electoral College selects the president.

When Washington arrived in New York City, he was greeted with parades and a thirteen-gun salute. He was sworn into office on the balcony of New York's Federal Hall. The crowds outside, obviously unsure about the difference between a president and a king, shouted, "Long live the president of the United States!" Hamilton and Eliza attended the inaugural ball. Washington wanted to be formal, but not kingly; open with the people, but not inappropriately familiar. In command on the battlefield but reserved and formal by nature, Washington leaned by nature toward appearing kingly, something he was afraid would set the wrong tone in a brand new republic. The new vice president, John Adams, adopted a royal style that outraged many, and which Washington carefully avoided. Washington asked Hamilton for advice on decorum. While Hamilton wanted the presidency to be infused with dignity, he encouraged Washington to be open to all visitors by offering weekly gatherings.

The most urgent problem facing the new president was the nation's finances. The Constitution made no mention of executive departments or of how the executive branch should be organized. Some congressmen thought the finances should be governed by a committee instead of an individual. Congress was terrified of giving too much power to the president and afraid that a single minister of finances in command of millions of dollars reporting only to the president created "power very unsafe in a republic."

After four months of political wrangling, Congress agreed that Washington had the power to create the Department of the Treasury and put a single person in charge. On September 11, 1789, Washington nominated Alexander Hamilton as secretary of the Treasury. Hamilton accepted. Everything was going his way. At last, he had the authority to try to fix the nation's finances. His father-in-law, Philip Schuyler, was a senator from New York.

James Madison, his ally in bringing about the new Constitution, was Speaker of the House.

Alexander Hamilton's commission as Treasury secretary, with George Washington's signature, 1789.

Hamilton plunged right in. On his very first day as secretary of the Treasury, he arranged for the federal government to borrow 50,000 dollars from the Bank of New York and, shortly afterward, applied for a 50,000-dollar loan from the Bank of North America. Within three weeks, he dispatched a letter to each customs inspector throughout the thirteen states requesting the exact figures of how much they collected each year on tariffs from goods entering the country.

When they sent back low numbers, he knew from his years in the Caribbean shipping industry exactly what was going on. Shippers were smuggling goods into the country to avoid tariffs. So with the money he borrowed, Hamilton established a national coast guard as part of the Treasury Department, which reduced the amount of goods brought illegally into the country. Soon tariff revenue flowed into United States coffers.

Congress asked Hamilton to report on his plans for dealing with the debt and establishing American credit abroad. They expected a modest proposal for reducing the war debt. For three months, Hamilton worked steadily, often late into the night. In January, Congress received a stunning 20,000-word treatise entitled *Report Relative to a Provision for the Support of Public Credit* that offered aggressive, far-reaching, and complex proposals. Part of Hamilton's plan was for the federal government to take over the war debts of the states and pay the foreign debt immediately in order to establish credibility so the new nation could borrow money. He referred to the war debt as "the price of liberty" and said that repaying it was the obligation of *all* Americans. Among the ways he intended to raise money to pay down the debt was by selling government securities, or bonds.

Hamilton's report was initially greeted with silence, most likely because reading the scholarly and densely written report and puzzling out what it meant was no easy task. Some members of Congress complained that Hamilton had deliberately made his proposal so complicated that nobody could comprehend it, allowing him to dupe everyone into approving something they didn't understand.

Soon Congress and the public figured out what Hamilton was up to: He was energetically and boldly using the potential power of the Treasury to build a strong central government. The resulting debate was furious and heated. In particular, there was enormous resistance to the federal government taking over state debt. Some of the northern states resisted, even though many of them were more heavily in debt, because they saw turning over their debt as the first step toward weakening themselves by empowering the central government. The southern states resisted pooling all the debt even more fiercely. They'd been less ravaged by the war and believed that pooling debt meant all states would share the burden equally. They didn't want to pay for debts incurred outside their state. Moreover, some states, such as Virginia, had already paid much of their own debt through hard work and sacrifice. Other aspects of Hamilton's plan generated fierce opposition as well, including the idea of selling securities, which prompted accusations that Hamilton was catering to the moneyed, merchant classes, looking for ways to help his New York City friends become wealthier.

Given the heated opposition to his report, Hamilton thought it prudent to wait before dropping his next bombshell: his intent to establish a central, national bank.

✶ ✶ ✶ ✶ ✶ ✶ ✶ ✶ ✶ ✶ ✶ ✶ ✶ ✶ ✶

Thomas Jefferson arrived in New York on March 21, 1790, to take up his new post as secretary of state. He and Hamilton were courteous to each other, fully aware that they were political opponents. In fact, Washington urged Jefferson to take the position of secretary of state because he wanted all regions and all viewpoints represented in his administration, and because Thomas Jefferson was an experienced statesman known throughout the world.

When Jefferson arrived, Hamilton was furiously lobbying Congress to accept his financial proposals, trying to persuade people to support him, offering bargains and intellectual arguments. He succeeded in convincing the states to pool their debt only after reaching a compromise with Jefferson: The new government would move the nation's capital to a southern site on the banks of the Potomac River adjacent to Virginia. In a compromise with Pennsylvanians, who fought hard to house the nation's capital, the Residence Act, passed in July, required Congress to move to Philadelphia until the new capital could be built. Pennsylvanians accepted the bargain, convinced that Philadelphia, already built and ready to accommodate the federal government, was so charming and appealing that once the government moved there, it would not want to leave. After the agreement was reached, Congress authorized Hamilton to have the federal government assume all the state debts and take steps to reduce the debt.

Afterward Jefferson insisted that he had been duped into supporting Hamilton's plans because he hadn't fully understood that

President George Washington in Consultation with His Secretary of State Thomas Jefferson and Secretary of the Treasury Alexander Hamilton, 1790. This mural by Constantino Brumidi is in the United States Senate reception room.

consolidating and taking control of the nation's debt was only Hamilton's first step in a grand scheme to use the national Treasury to consolidate power in the federal government.

Jefferson watched, appalled and alarmed, as Hamilton used the national debt to justify creating a bureaucracy that reached into all corners of the new republic, touching the lives of ordinary Americans through the power of government spending. Jefferson shouldn't have been surprised. Hamilton had openly stated his belief that a national debt "will be a powerful cement of our union. It will also create a necessity for keeping up taxation to a degree which, without being oppressive, will be a spur to industry." Moreover, Hamilton had commented in the *Federalist Papers* that because people are creatures of habit, the more they become accustomed to having the government as part of their everyday lives, the more affection they would have for their government, in turn giving the government credibility and stabilizing the nation.

When the capital moved to Philadelphia, Hamilton opened the United States Department of the Treasury at 100 Chestnut Street. He relocated his family to the city, which was then the political and cultural center of America. The waterfront streets were home to the state's most prominent families. Hamilton rented a house at 79 South Third Street, not far from the most elegant neighborhoods. Hamilton and Eliza were now parents to a fourth child, James, born in 1788. Hamilton and Eliza were often invited to dinner parties and lavish balls hosted by the city's elite. Hamilton, always at ease in social gatherings, was frequently seen relaxing at the card table, or at the theater with Eliza.

He sought none of the trappings of power. During the workday, he labored at the Treasury office, in a room that was almost bare. He sat at a plain pine table covered with a green cloth, his books and papers piled on makeshift shelves. A Frenchman who visited his office remarked that the entire furnishings of the Department of the Treasury could not be worth more than ten dollars.

✶ ✶ ✶ ✶ ✶ ✶ ✶ ✶ ✶ ✶ ✶ ✶ ✶ ✶ ✶

Buried in Hamilton's *Report Relative to a Provision for the Support of Public Credit* was a proposal for a new tax. He knew the people wouldn't like it. In an agricultural society in which most families met all their own needs, people saw little point in sending money to a distant government. Besides, the Revolutionary War had been largely fought over taxes, with the result that many Americans associated the word "taxes" with a government out to steal from them. So he cast about for a tax that would be least unpopular and hit on the idea of a "sin" tax

---

on whiskey, also called a "luxury" tax, to be paid by the producers of whiskey. Privately he told Washington that he wanted to tax whiskey before the states got the idea.

He waited until the end of 1790 to ask Congress to impose the whiskey tax. Not surprisingly, there was vehement anger. Southern states warned that they would simply ignore the tax. Others called a federal tax an act of war on the citizens. The very next day, while everyone was still reeling from the idea of a new federal tax, Hamilton announced his intention to create a national bank. His bank proposal caused such an uproar that the whiskey tax slipped through Congress propelled by Hamilton's allies and supporters. Because at that time Hamilton didn't take steps to collect the tax, it went mostly unnoticed.

His bank proposal was to start with ten million dollars—five times more than the worth of all banks in America put together. One-fifth would come from the federal government, and the remainder from the sale of stock. He wanted federal funds deposited into the bank, which would then offer bank notes—or paper money—to provide a uniform currency throughout all thirteen states. The bank could lend money to the federal government in emergencies and offer loans to private individuals to "promote national prosperity." He explained that such a bank would serve as a nursery for wealth.

Hamilton's suggestion was greeted with joy from America's mercantile class, but triggered fear in others. Thomas Jefferson said such a bank was an engine for swindling and corruption. Hamilton tried to explain that funded debt—meaning debt in the form of securities—along with a central bank would allow the government to have a source of money other than taxes. He promised that the bank would be carefully regulated so it would operate as a tool for the public good.

These reassurances didn't help. Jefferson and others were alarmed by what they believed to be Hamilton's scheme to turn America into another Great Britain, seeing a national bank as a vehicle for kingly wealth and power. To Jefferson, by enriching the central government, Hamilton was demolishing liberty, robbing states of their independence, and undermining the main pillar of democracy—that the people should govern themselves. Hamilton, on the other hand, envisioned America taking its place among the leading empires of the world—and that required money and a bank.

When Hamilton's proposal for a bank sailed through Congress, mostly because of his allies, Jefferson pinned his hopes on Washington, a fellow Virginian who, he believed, would understand the dangers of enlarging the government. He handed the president a written argument that Hamilton's bank violated the

Constitution. Jefferson's argument was that there was nothing in the Constitution that gave the federal government the power to establish a federal bank. Therefore, according to Jefferson, Hamilton's plan was unconstitutional.

Washington, unsure about what to do, gave Jefferson's brief to Hamilton and asked for a response. While Jefferson had quickly dashed off his arguments, Hamilton labored to craft his answer, which ended up ten times longer than Jefferson's objections. In his response, Hamilton assured Washington that a federal bank *was* constitutional. After all, Hamilton said, the Constitution charged the executive branch with recommending to Congress any measures it believed were "necessary and proper," and Congress had the power to pass "all laws which shall be necessary and proper."

The preamble to the Constitution, the introductory paragraph that sets out the principles underlying the entire document, reads:

We the people of the United States, in order to form a more perfect union, establish justice, insure domestic tranquility, provide for the common defense, promote the general welfare, and secure the blessings of liberty to ourselves and our posterity, do ordain and establish this Constitution for the United States of America.

THE CONSTITUTION contains a great many words and phrases that are vague and morally charged, such as "necessary and proper," "general welfare," and "liberty." People are inclined to read into these phrases whatever ideas they have to start with. What, for example, does "liberty" mean? The slave owners believed liberty meant they had the freedom to own slaves, even though this meant depriving others of *their* freedom. Given that the Constitution is filled with so many vague words and phrases, the question immediately arose: How should the Constitution be interpreted?

Beginning as early as the *Federalist Papers*, Hamilton advocated a loose interpretation that would allow flexibility under the Constitution. He understood that the Constitution resulted from compromises, including the compromise about slavery, and he expected—or perhaps hoped—that over time, Americans would have different

Hamilton argued that because a bank would "promote the general welfare," the Constitution fully empowered the legislative and executive branches to establish a bank.

ideas about liberty and freedom. Seeing the Constitution as ironclad would hinder growth and change, forever freezing the country as it stood in 1787.

The originalist view, put forward by Thomas Jefferson, held that the Constitution must be read exactly as it was intended, and any proposed change must go through the cumbersome amendment process. According to the originalists, allowing for a loose interpretation would result in lack of stability because everyone would have a different idea of what the words *should* mean. Originalists also understood that interpreting the Constitution loosely would enable the federal government to grow. Jefferson suggested that anyone trying to decide what the Constitution meant should "carry themselves back" to the time when it was adopted and "recollect the spirit manifested in the debates," instead of inventing a new meaning with each change in the culture.

Hamilton's argument—that the "necessary and proper" and "general welfare" clauses allowed for a federal bank—struck Jefferson as making things up, reading into the Constitution things that weren't there and were never intended. If people could read in anything they wanted, what was the point of a constitution in the first place?

Washington spent a full day considering Jefferson's argument and Hamilton's rebuttal. Then he sided with Hamilton.

For some time, Jefferson had been irked that Washington most often turned to Hamilton for advice, even in matters that seemed to Jefferson beyond the scope of the Treasury. The result was that ambassadors from Europe frequently mistook Hamilton for a prime minister, despite the fact that Jefferson was fourteen years older and a far more experienced statesman. Jefferson believed Washington had been seduced and beguiled by the corrupt and wily Hamilton. Jefferson felt himself bested not by Hamilton's intellect but by what he saw as Hamilton's political savvy.

✺ ✺ ✺ ✺ ✺ ✺ ✺ ✺ ✺ ✺ ✺ ✺ ✺ ✺ ✺

Hamilton submitted a lengthy proposal to Washington and Congress for using the Treasury to encourage the growth of industry and manufacturing by means of regulations to increase productivity and reward innovation. The *Report on the Subject of Manufactures*, one of Hamilton's lengthiest and most complete proposals, predicted that America would become a great industrial nation and explained how to get there. While Hamilton acknowledged the obvious importance of farming, he believed industry and manufacturing were better sources of wealth. There were limits to how much a plot of land could produce, but as industry and technology improved, production could increase. To promote trade and industry, he proposed a giant system of roadways and canals to link different parts of the country and reduce transportation costs. He wanted to encourage immigration of skilled workers and enforce standards on American products. He justified his building plan by relying on the "public welfare" phrase in the Constitution.

Jefferson was again horrified by Hamilton's plan, particularly because it relied so heavily on a subjective interpretation of a single phrase in the Constitution. He was determined to fight fire with fire. He understood that Hamilton's success came about because he'd assembled a group of allies and supporters who called themselves Federalists—the start of America's first political party. So he encouraged a friend and well-respected journalist to start a newspaper dedicated to denouncing Hamilton's schemes. He traveled to New York and met with Governor Clinton. Together, he and Clinton rallied all those opposed to Alexander Hamilton, forming a political party to rival the Federalists. Jefferson's party came to be called the Democratic-

Republicans, the forerunner of today's Democratic Party.

George Washington, saddened by the growing factions, thought political parties were baneful and divisive. But there was nothing he could do to prevent them from forming. The lines were clearly drawn, with the Democratic-Republicans struggling to hold on to state sovereignty and the Federalists pushing for a strong, centralized government. The Federalists generally represented the interests of merchants and city dwellers, while the Democratic-Republicans drew their strength from the rural countryside.

★ ★ ★ ★ ★ ★ ★ ★ ★ ★ ★ ★ ★ ★ ★

The quarrel between the originalists and the nonoriginalists continues to this day, with originalists seeking to interpret the Constitution as intended in 1787, and nonoriginalists pointing out that because so many different people contributed to the Constitution, which was the result of compromises, how can anyone determine intention? Besides, much of what the framers intended is not acceptable to most Americans today. Most of the framers, for example, thought only white men should have a voice in government. "We the people," as the nonoriginalists today point out, did not originally include all people. Many Americans today would have no wish to return to America as it stood in 1787.

II

Rivalry with Jefferson

*'Tis the malicious intrigues to stab me in
the dark, against which I am too often obliged
to guard myself, distract and harass me . . .*

— Alexander Hamilton

amilton and his Federalist allies suffered their first
defeat in 1791, when Aaron Burr, in a heated election,
took Philip Schuyler's seat in the Senate, winning the
election with the help of the Clintons and the other
Democratic-Republicans. It was a blow to Hamilton,
who relied on his father-in-law in the Senate to help pass his proposals through Congress. The fact that Burr, who had been born in New
Jersey, had achieved political prominence in New York was a testa-
ment to his talents as a politician. New York was then dominated

by three leading families, the Clintons, the Livingstons, and the Schuylers. Outsiders had a hard time breaking in. In the words of one historian, "The Clintons had *power*, the Livingstons had *numbers*, and the Schuylers had *Hamilton*." For Philip Schuyler to be ousted by someone who hailed from outside the state was a shock to Hamilton.

As the end of George Washington's first term drew near, Washington gave in to the pleadings of almost everyone, including both Jefferson and Hamilton, and agreed to run for another term. Jefferson and Hamilton agreed that only the prestige of Washington could hold together the warring factions. There were questions, though, of who would be the next vice president.

When the Democratic-Republicans put forward Aaron Burr as a possible replacement for John Adams, Hamilton coordinated a campaign against Burr—who lost to John Adams.

✶ ✶ ✶ ✶ ✶ ✶ ✶ ✶ ✶ ✶ ✶ ✶ ✶ ✶ ✶

By Washington's second term as president, Hamilton had completely turned around the nation's finances. Along with establishing a bank and the coast guard, he'd devised a complete set of procedures for handling and reporting revenue and debt. Prices were steady, the value of American currency was strong, and businesses were perking up and even prospering.

In some areas—particularly in the northern cities that were
emerging as centers of commerce and trade—money flowed so
freely that Jefferson and his allies became convinced there must
be foul play. Democratic-Republicans accused Hamilton of corruption and mishandling public funds. In the view of those who
didn't understand mercantilism, there was no other explanation
for how people without farms suddenly got money they didn't
have before. William Branch Giles, a Virginia congressman,
introduced five resolutions to Congress asserting that Hamilton
had submitted false reports and had failed to account for a million dollars. The Virginians and others, fully believing Hamilton
and his allies were dipping their hands into the funds, called for
him to resign.

Hamilton was hurt and shocked, particularly when he learned
that James Madison, his former ally, was involved. Hamilton
responded to the accusations by marshaling his entire staff to
prepare lengthy and comprehensive reports tracing every penny
that had passed through the Department of the Treasury since
the day the doors opened. It took one full month for Hamilton's staff to assemble the entire history of the Treasury into
a gargantuan report for Congress. Those who had the patience
to work through the stacks of papers concluded that there had

been no wrongdoing—every penny was accounted for, and there was no evidence that Hamilton had done anything illegal. When Hamilton was found completely innocent, Jefferson was aghast, convinced that inquiry had been biased and the judging not fair.

In fact, Hamilton's personal financial situation was deteriorating in the service of his country. Unlike other government officials—who kept their law practices active, or who had independent wealth, or who, like Jefferson, owned a large plantation—Hamilton was falling into debt, unable to maintain his family's lifestyle on his government salary. He worked such grueling hours in the Treasury Department that he simply didn't have time to represent private clients as well. Bitter and frustrated, he felt that he was dedicating his life to his country and being repaid with false accusations and venom. The strain of defending himself against the accusations wore him out so much that he was continually sick.

Hamilton and Jefferson no longer made any attempts to be polite. They sniped at each other so incessantly that Washington took to meeting with each of his secretaries

Thomas Jefferson, 1800,
by Rembrandt Peale.

without the other present, and often pleaded with them in vain to mend their differences and come together for the good of the country.

When an outbreak of the deadly yellow fever swept through Philadelphia, both Hamilton and Eliza became ill. The children, who remained healthy, were moved to an adjoining house. Eliza calmed the frantic children by waving to them from a window. Hamilton's boyhood friend, Edward Stevens, now a doctor, was in Philadelphia treating patients, and was able to tend to both Eliza and Hamilton. Within five days, both improved. To complete their recovery, they left Philadelphia and journeyed to Albany to recuperate in the Schuyler mansion. In one of his meaner moments, Jefferson wrote to James Madison, accusing Hamilton of faking his illness as a cowardly way of gaining sympathy.

Hamilton was ready to resign his post, but Washington persuaded him to come back to work. So after he and Eliza fully recovered, they returned to Philadelphia, and Hamilton resumed his duties as secretary of the Treasury.

✳ ✳ ✳ ✳ ✳ ✳ ✳ ✳ ✳ ✳ ✳ ✳ ✳ ✳ ✳

Hamilton didn't expect the whiskey tax to be popular, but he also didn't expect farmers to attack the tax collectors, beating, tarring and feathering, and running them out of town on a rail. The farmers, having won the Revolutionary War against the British, understood that they lived in a democracy, which to them meant that the people governed themselves, and which they felt gave them not only the right but the obligation to fight back against an oppressive government. What could be more oppressive than a tax collector from Philadelphia demanding money on each bottle of whiskey they sold? Hamilton was galled when Albert Gallatin, a member of the Pennsylvania Assembly who would later be elected to the Senate, encouraged Pennsylvanians to treat the tax and tax collectors with contempt in the name of democracy.

For Hamilton, a government—even a democratic one—required law and order. He didn't think democracy meant people had the right to beat up tax collectors. Beating up tax collectors and rejecting laws duly passed by Congress was, to him, pure anarchy and a challenge to the legitimacy of government.

Hamilton and Washington agreed to make peace by lessening the whiskey tax burden, particularly for small country distillers, and shifting the burden to imported whiskey. Once these changes were made, they sent peacemakers to Western Pennsylvania. These measures succeeded—but only temporarily. There were still taxes to be paid. Reports of violence trickled back to Philadelphia. First irate distillers threatened inspectors, and then farmers attacked distillers who complied with the law.

When six thousand insurgents converged outside Pittsburgh, Washington issued a proclamation ordering them to back down, or the federal government would send in a militia. After much wrangling and failed negotiations, Washington called for a militia. Hamilton, wearing full military dress, rode with Washington at the head of the soldiers. They reached Pittsburgh to find that the outlaws had dispersed and couldn't be found. Even though locals refused to furnish information about the rebels, two men were tried and found guilty of treason. Washington pardoned them both.

The new Democratic-Republican newspaper severely criticized Hamilton and Washington, accusing them of behaving exactly like the British in using force to collect taxes. They called Hamilton a warmonger who would stop at nothing—even turning an army on the American people—to defend his corrupt policies. Hamilton blamed the uprising on Jefferson and the Democratic-Republicans and their cavalier attitude toward rebellion.

Three days after returning from Western Pennsylvania, Hamilton informed the president and Speaker of the House that he would resign on January 31, 1795. Eliza had recently suffered a miscarriage, and she was still feeling ill. Hamilton felt he needed to return to his private law practice for the good of his family. His debts then exceeded his assets, and he worried that if he died, his wife and children—by then he had six, including Fanny—would be dependent upon others. From the moment he married Eliza, he'd vowed never to rely on her family's fortunes. He'd gotten his

nation's finances in order. Now he felt it was time to return to a private law practice and get his own finances in better shape. He estimated that after practicing law for five years, he'd be on his feet again.

The Whiskey Rebellion, c. 1795, attributed to Frederick Kemmelmeyer, showing Washington and his troops near Fort Cumberland, Maryland, before their march to suppress the rebellion.

In February, when his resignation became effective, he returned with his family to New York and was hailed as a hero by the merchant community. The chamber of commerce hosted a dinner attended by two hundred people, excluding others who wanted to attend but couldn't because the room wasn't large enough. After a rest in Albany at the Schuyler mansion, the Hamiltons returned to New York City. They rented a home at 26 Broadway, and Hamilton returned to his private law practice.

The moment he opened his law office, he had more work than he could handle. He was soon the city's most prominent lawyer. His clients included all the wealthiest and most influential men in the city, and the most prosperous businesses. His fees were modest, but he had so much work that his income was soon three to four times what he had earned as secretary of the Treasury.

Happy to be away from government service, he turned down requests to run for office. When John Jay, then governor of New York, offered Hamilton a newly vacated Senate seat, Hamilton refused. He kept himself informed of all matters of government, though, and remained influential. George Washington still turned to him for advice. When unsure what to do about a sticky issue, he wrote to Hamilton to find out what he thought.

In 1796, George Washington, too, was ready to retire. He was sixty-four and resisted pleas to remain president for another term. Eager to return to his Mount Vernon home, he famously said he was ready to retire under his own vine and fig tree.

He asked both Madison and Hamilton to help with his farewell statement to the American people. Madison did a first draft, and Hamilton helped revise, edit, and shape the final version—which bore Hamilton's unmistakable voice and the Federalist ideals that he and Washington had come to share. The address opened with Washington's reasons for retiring, explaining that "choice and prudence invite me to quit the political scene." He urged the citizens to keep the union strong, encouraging them to think of themselves first as Americans:

> The name of American, which belongs to you in your national capacity, must always exalt the just pride of patriotism more than any appellation derived from local distinctions.

Jefferson and the Democratic-Republicans, not knowing that Hamilton had actually drafted the final version of the address, were deeply saddened that their beloved George Washington had been so thoroughly seduced and hoodwinked by the Federalists.

12

Rivalry with Burr

*Every day proves to me more
and more that this American world
was not made for me.*

— Alexander Hamilton

ew York, rebuilt and recovered from the war, was emerging as the nation's center of commerce and business. But the city's water was foul, vile-smelling, and believed to be the cause of a series of deadly outbreaks of yellow fever. After one devastating outbreak in 1799 that killed as many as forty-five people per day, Aaron Burr, who was then a member of the New York Assembly, submitted a report from Dr. Joseph Browne, his brother-in-law, confirming that contaminated water was causing

the disease. Burr also submitted a plan for a new waterworks, chartered by the state legislature, that would provide fresh water and meet the other needs of the city, such as water to fight fires and clean the streets.

The city council adopted the proposal. The state was prepared

Aaron Burr, 1802, by John Vanderlyn.

to undertake the project, but Burr changed what he was asking for, and argued instead that a private company should manage the project. To convince everyone that he sincerely wished to save the state money, he asked six men to serve on his committee, three Federalists and three Democratic-Republicans. He approached Hamilton and asked him to serve. Hamilton, appalled that contaminated city water was causing so many deaths, readily agreed. He drafted the charter for the private waterworks, and he wrote a memo to the state legislature support-ing the project. Hamilton's name gave the project gave instant credibility, and Burr had no problem getting the charter approved.

What Hamilton didn't know was that after Burr submitted the charter, he made a few changes. He deleted provisions promising to provide free water to combat fires in the city. More importantly, he slipped in a provision that allowed the private water company to use surplus capital to purchase public or other stocks. The effect of this provision was that the waterworks company, called the Manhattan Company, became a private bank controlled by Burr.

The charter allowed the Manhattan Company to instantly raise two million dollars and open up directorships that Burr gave to his fellow Democratic-Republicans. Because Hamilton had drafted the charter as if the Manhattan Company would be a waterworks company, the bank had much more freedom than a bank would ordinarily have. Shares in the Manhattan Company were priced at only fifty dollars, much lower than shares in the Bank of New York, which made them accessible to ordinary middle-class citizens. The day Manhattan Company shares went on sale, they sold out immediately.

Hamilton was enraged when he learned that Burr had duped him. Hamilton knew right away why Burr had fooled everyone: The Federalist-controlled government would have never given Burr permission to charter a bank, and the Democratic-Republicans would view any Democratic-Republican able to get a foothold into New York banking as a hero.

It wasn't long before Hamilton exacted his revenge for being duped. Burr was up for reelection for the assembly that very month. Hamilton made sure the voters understood what Burr had done. The voters, it turned out, were as angry as Hamilton. In the same month stocks in the Manhattan Company went up for sale, Burr was voted out of office.

By the time the Manhattan Company opened its doors on Wall Street in September, it no longer kept up the pretense of being a water company. The Manhattan Company did very little about the water situation. It never piped in water from the Bronx River, as promised. Instead, the company dug new wells in what is now SoHo. Yellow fever outbreaks continued in New York.

Just before the Manhattan Company bank opened, two men— one of the bank directors and John Church, Hamilton's brother-in-law—accused Burr of accepting bribes. Burr responded by challenging Church to a duel. The day after the bank opened, the two men rowed across the river to the dueling grounds. The duel began the usual way, with both men measuring the distance between them. Both missed their first shots, at which point Church apologized, saying his remark had been indiscreet. The men shook hands and called off the duel, a common way for a duel to end. It was an eerie prelude to the deadly duel that would take place five years later between Hamilton and Burr.

THE MANHATTAN COMPANY BANK
is still in existence today. After several mergers, first
with Chase Bank and then with J.P. Morgan & Co.,
the Manhattan Company came to be called JPMorgan
Chase. The bank that began as Aaron Burr's ruse
against Alexander Hamilton is now America's largest
bank, with 2.5 trillion dollars in assets.

In December 1799, George Washington died in his bed after a
brief illness. Hamilton was devastated. He wrote to Martha Washington, "No one, better than myself, knows the greatness of your
loss, or how much your excellent heart is formed to feel it in all its
extent," and described how Washington's confidence and friendship had made so much possible for him. Indeed, Washington had
allowed Hamilton to rise to greatness. By a strange coincidence,
Hamilton's father died the same year in obscurity in the Caribbean, although it's unlikely Hamilton knew of his death. As if to
nearly complete the trilogy of dying father figures in Hamilton's
life, Philip Schuyler, who adored his brilliant son-in-law and who
was the closest Hamilton had to a real father, was growing ill and
infirm, and Hamilton feared he would soon lose Philip as well.

✳ ✳ ✳ ✳ ✳ ✳ ✳ ✳ ✳ ✳ ✳ ✳ ✳ ✳ ✳

After Washington left office, the Democratic-Republicans found ways to systematically weaken the central government and empower the states. When Virginia and Kentucky adopted resolutions stating that the Constitution was merely a contract between the states and that states were free to ignore federal laws they believed were unconstitutional, Hamilton felt the union was on the verge of unraveling. He didn't think it would take much to bring about its complete collapse. "Every moment's reflection," he wrote to a friend, "increases my chagrin and disgust."

Hamilton's behavior during the 1800 election struck many of his friends as completely unhinged. John Adams, a Federalist, was running for a second term. His chief opponents were Thomas Jefferson and Aaron Burr. Hamilton became passionately convinced that Adams must not win reelection, despite the fact that he had served as vice president for both of Washington's presidential terms and was at least nominally a Federalist.

Adams and Hamilton had never liked each other. Adams resented Hamilton for occupying the position of Washington's closest adviser, a position he felt should have been his, as vice president. Adams had once circulated a myth that Hamilton was at the head of a pro-British faction. Adams called Hamilton a lowborn foreigner—the "bastard brat of a Scotch peddler." It was a slight Hamilton never forgot or forgave. For Hamilton, though, it was a matter of Adams's fitness to lead. He genuinely believed that Adams was not up to governing the country. He issued a publication entitled "Letter from Alexander Hamilton, Concerning the Public Conduct and Character of John Adams" and let loose a series of attacks. Hamilton campaigned for another Federalist, Charles Cotesworth Pinckney, which weakened the Federalist Party and split the Federalist vote.

Because the Democratic-Republicans were unified and better organized, the top two finishers, Burr and Jefferson, were both Democratic-Republicans. When the voting by the Electoral College was tallied, Burr and Jefferson were tied. The outgoing House of Representatives had the job of breaking the tie, but they couldn't do it. After dozens of rounds of voting, neither Jefferson nor Burr had a majority. The problem was that each state's House delegation had only one vote, and Maryland and Vermont were deadlocked and thus could not vote. Most Federalists preferred Burr to Jefferson, and Congress was leaning toward Burr. If Hamilton had remained silent, Burr would likely have become the third president of the United States. But Hamilton wasn't about to remain silent. He and

Jefferson had long been political opponents and even enemies. In fact, Jefferson was campaigning on a promise to repeal Hamilton's whiskey tax, but Hamilton knew Jefferson to be an honest man of principle. Burr, in Hamilton's opinion, had no redeeming qualities.

The House of Representatives went through more rounds of voting, and each time neither candidate received the necessary majority. Meanwhile, Hamilton was doing all he could to throw the election to Jefferson. He insisted that Jefferson "is by far not so dangerous a man and he has pretensions to character," not a ringing endorsement, perhaps, but Burr, he said, was worse: a man without any principles at all.

On the thirty-sixth vote, enough congressmen in deadlocked states switched their votes to Jefferson so that he finally won by a narrow margin. Burr lost—and held Hamilton responsible. Jefferson became president and Burr vice president.

After Adams left office, the Federalists never again won the presidency. Hamilton has been called a fool for playing a part in smashing his own party. Hamilton justified his refusal to endorse either Adams or Burr by saying that the public good was more important than loyalty to a party. Yes, he had helped build the Federalist Party, but he had also helped create the United States, and the country was dearer to him than his party.

Thomas Jefferson struck a peacemaking tone in his inaugural address, calling for harmony between the warring political parties. He said, "We are all Republicans; we are all Federalists." Once in office, he confirmed Hamilton's beliefs that he would make a better president than Burr. He governed as a principled moderate. He adopted many of Hamilton's policies, even using Hamilton's own constitutional law arguments—the ones Hamilton had once used against him—to justify federal authority to make the Louisiana Purchase, an acquisition of 828,000 square miles of territory from the Mississippi River to the Rocky Mountains. The Louisiana Purchase was criticized by many states rights' advocates as an abuse of federal power. Nothing in the Constitution, after all, authorized such a purchase. Jefferson loosely interpreted the Constitution in the spirit of the nonoriginalists, arguing that the clause giving the federal government the power to enter into treaties also gave it the power to make land purchases.

Without the Treasury Department and national credit Hamilton had built, the purchase would not have been possible.

★ ★ ★ ★ ★ ★ ★ ★ ★ ★ ★ ★ ★ ★ ★

s Hamilton had predicted, five years in private practice as a lawyer gave him the means to buy a piece of land

and build a family house. By then he and Eliza had eight children. He selected a site in the north part of Manhattan, a place he and Eliza had fallen in love with for its wooded country and nearby fishing pond. The property was nine miles from Hamilton's law office, a ninety-minute trip in his day, difficult for a lawyer practicing in the city but removed from the frequent outbreaks of yellow fever. Because of the hardships of the commute, even after the house was built, he kept his rental house in the city.

He oversaw the building of the home, a two-story mansion painted yellow and ivory with sun porches on two sides. Parlor

The Grange, Hamilton's home, date and artist unknown.

windows offered a view of the Hudson River. The first thing visitors saw when they entered was a portrait of George Washington.

Hamilton called his home the Grange, a name that recalled his Scottish descendants, for that was the name of his father's home in Scotland. The name also recalled his boyhood on St. Croix because his mother's family's plantation had also been called the Grange. He never spoke in public of his ancestry or his boyhood, but now as a man of forty-six, he honored his roots.

When one of his friends complained that there wasn't a decent newspaper in New York City representing the Federalist viewpoint, Hamilton founded one. He put up part of the money to get the paper started and helped hire the editor. The masthead of the newspaper, evoking Jefferson's moderate tone, announced that although the views leaned Federalist, the editor recognized that both parties had honest, virtuous men and good ideas. The *New York Evening Post* became one of the country's most successful newspapers and is still published today under the name the *New York Post*.

While Hamilton didn't take part in the daily operation of the paper, the editor, William Coleman, explained that whenever he needed to write about a topic but he didn't have enough information, he simply called on Hamilton, who would instantly dictate the article. Coleman wrote quickly as Hamilton spoke, and when Hamilton finished speaking, Coleman's article was complete.

In an interesting twist, Hamilton, who had always been painted by his enemies as opposed to individual liberty in favor of a strong government, defended the rights of individual freedom against President Thomas Jefferson. The case arose when President Jefferson brought charges against a small newspaper in Hudson, New York, called the *Wasp*, for running an unflattering article about him. The article accused Jefferson, among other things, of rewarding people for calling George Washington a traitor. The *Wasp* was known to be deliberately provocative, its stated purpose to "lash the rascals" of the world.

Jefferson accused the *Wasp*'s editor, Croswell, of libel—writing and publishing an article that damaged Jefferson's reputation. The charge was that Croswell "wickedly and maliciously" harmed Jefferson's reputation and undermined public confidence in the president of the United States. A person whose reputation was damaged by libel could sue under the common law theory that one person shouldn't be able to destroy the character of another. Also under common law, a person claiming to be libeled needed only to prove that the statements had damaged his reputation. It didn't matter whether the statements were true.

THE BILL OF RIGHTS—the first ten amendments to the Constitution—was ratified in 1791, four years after the signing of the Constitution, and included the First Amendment's guarantee of freedom of speech and the press: "Congress shall make no law . . . abridging the freedom of speech, or of the press." The language of the First Amendment appears straightforward. But upon closer inspection, the phrase "Congress shall make no law" complicates matters because the lawsuit against the *Wasp* was filed under New York law. Congress had made no law abridging the *Wasp*, so at least on the surface there was nothing in the Constitution to prevent Jefferson from suing for libel. At the same time, Jefferson—as the president of the United States—represented the government. The First Amendment was further complicated by the fact that, under common law, some forms of speech were not allowed. Libel and slander had always been unlawful. Other forms of speech were unlawful as well, such as shouting "Fire" in a crowded building if there is no fire.

The task of defining the limits of the First Amendment fell to the courts.

Hamilton agreed to defend the newspaper against the charge of libel, working without compensation because Croswell was unable to pay a fee. He argued that the truth should be a defense in accusations of libel; otherwise there would be nothing to stop tyrants. He gained sympathy for his argument by appealing to the very ideals over which the Revolutionary War had been fought. He argued that in a democracy—as opposed to a monarchy—the press had an obligation to report bad behavior of those in office so the public could make informed decisions. To this day, *People v. Croswell* stands as a landmark case for freedom of the press.

✳ ✳ ✳ ✳ ✳ ✳ ✳ ✳ ✳ ✳ ✳ ✳ ✳ ✳ ✳

While Hamilton's house was being built, an incident occurred that sank Hamilton into a depression from which he never recovered. His oldest son, Philip, then twenty years old and a recent graduate of Columbia, was the most gifted of Hamilton's children. He was also an impulsive and rambunctious young man who tended to get himself into trouble. One evening he got into a heated argument with a Democratic-Republican at the Park Theater in New York. The quarrel started when Philip and his friend mocked a young lawyer, George Eacker, who had recently given a speech excoriating the Federalists and

Alexander Hamilton. Eacker challenged Philip to a duel, and Philip accepted. They met on the dueling ground in Weehawken in New Jersey. Eacker took careful aim and shot Philip. Philip fell, never having fired a shot. Mortally wounded, he was carried home. His family, frantic, gathered around him. He died within hours.

The entire family sank into a deep and inconsolable grief. Eliza was then three months pregnant with the child who would turn out to be their last. Her shock and anguish endangered her health and the unborn child. Hamilton fell into such despair he was never the same again. Friends said that grief for his son became permanently etched into his face.

★ ★ ★ ★ ★ ★ ★ ★ ★ ★ ★ ★ ★ ★ ★

Hamilton should have been able to retire, basking in his accomplishments and the knowledge that the nation he helped build was thriving. The Louisiana Purchase had doubled the size of the country. The nation's finances were so strong that the Louisiana Purchase could be shrugged off at a mere fifteen million dollars. But he couldn't rest. He remained terrified that the nation would come undone by men who pledged greater allegiance to their state or region than to the republic. In a letter to a good friend, Gouverneur Morris, he wrote:

Mine is an odd destiny. Perhaps no man in the United States has sacrificed or done more for the present Constitution than myself–and contrary to all my anticipations of its fate, as you know from the very beginning I am still laboring to prop the frail and worthless fabric.

Hamilton felt depressed when Jefferson, although in many ways a moderate, put an end to plans to build a national highway system. Most alarming, though, was a movement in New England to secede from the union on the grounds that the Louisiana Purchase so enlarged the country that New England would become insignificant, its voice powerless. The New Englanders were led by Roger Griswold, a Connecticut lawyer and congressman, and Timothy Pickering, who'd once been a good friend of Hamilton's and part of George Washington's administration. The northerners chafed at a president who was a southerner and slaveholder, and worried that the Louisiana Purchase would become a slave-holding region, making them part of a country led by those whose values they despised. The New England secessionists came up with a plan to break off from the union and perhaps join with people in south Canada to form a country with close alliances to Britain. They approached Hamilton, hoping to persuade New York to join them. Hamilton refused.

So instead they approached Aaron Burr, who they viewed as more malleable. The next presidential election was approaching, and Burr knew he had no chance at either the presidency or the vice presidency. Jefferson was the favorite for reelection. He and Burr had never gotten along. Now that the Twelfth Amendment had changed how vice presidents were selected, Jefferson could drop Burr as vice president and choose George Clinton instead.

The New England secessionists formed a plan to get Burr elected governor of New York and make New York the center of the Northern Confederacy. The plan seemed plausible because a large number of New Yorkers in the upstate rural areas still had no wish to be part of a large union.

Hamilton responded by doing everything he could to make sure Burr lost the election for governor. Hamilton's unbounded energy to attack Burr came partly from a fear that Burr, if elected governor, would indeed join New England in seceding from the union. He gave heated speeches vilifying Burr as a corrupt and unprincipled schemer. He begged New Yorkers to avoid the disaster of a Burr governorship. Hamilton was not the only Federalist campaigning hard against Burr. Others called Burr "dishonest and fraudulent" and "a man destitute of moral virtue, and bent solely on the gratification of his passions, regardless of the public good."

At a private dinner, Hamilton and a friend, New York Supreme Court Justice James Kent, were discussing Burr. Another guest at the table was Dr. Charles Cooper, who afterward wrote a letter to Philip Schuyler describing the dinner table talk. "Hamilton and Judge Kent have declared in substance, that they looked upon Mr. Burr to be a dangerous man and one who ought not to be trusted with the reins of government," he wrote. The letter ended up printed in an Albany newspaper.

Burr lost the election for governor in a landslide. He still had ten months left in his term as vice president of the United States. Ordinarily, Burr was unflappable. Now, after his defeat, he was bitter and angry and off balance. He was still in the throes of fury when someone showed him the newspaper article containing Hamilton's remarks about him.

A heated series of letters and messages passed between Hamilton and Burr. When their friends were unable to patch up the quarrel, Burr challenged Hamilton to a duel, and Hamilton accepted.

⓭

Afterward

When the word spread that Hamilton was dead from a bullet wound inflicted by Burr, the outpouring of grief and shock was intense and genuine. Crowds, weeping, gathered in front of his downtown house. A stunned and mournful silence descended on the city. All business stopped. Messages of condolence poured in from across the country and Europe. People wore black bands of mourning. Ships in the harbor, both foreign and American, lowered their flags to half-mast.

Alexander Hamilton after his duel with Aaron Burr, date and artist unknown.

The New York Common Council paid for a state funeral. On the day of the funeral, Saturday, July 14, 1804, muffled church bells rang morning, noon, and night. A vast funeral procession, consisting of the governor and mayor, congressmen and civil officers, military officers, bankers, lawyers, and students of law, moved solemnly through the city. Gouverneur Morris delivered the eulogy on a platform in front of Trinity Church in lower Manhattan. At his feet were all of Hamilton's children, except for the youngest, who was then two years old.

The scheme for some of the northern states to secede died along with Hamilton. Some historians say that the scheme died because of Hamilton's death—those who remained could not enter a plot that Hamilton had died to prevent. Others say that the scheme had never been a serious threat to the union.

Thomas Jefferson, in homage to his former adversary, installed a bust of Hamilton at his home in Monticello, where it occupied a place of honor in the entrance hall. He positioned the bust of Hamilton across from a bust of himself. Visitors to Monticello today can see the bust of Jefferson and a replica of the bust of Hamilton on display.

Burr emerged as a public villain. One New York newspaper declared that Hamilton had been slain by an assassin. A South

Carolina newspaper speculated that Burr's heart must be filled with cinders from the fires of hell. Burr was shocked to receive death threats. People called for the hanging of the vice president. New Jersey indicted Burr for murder, but tossed out the charges because Hamilton died in New York. New York also indicted him for murder, then reduced the charges to a misdemeanor for dueling, but that charge never went to trial.

In the words of one historian, the bullet that killed Hamilton also killed Burr. Driven into exile, Burr headed to the western territories, where he reportedly told Andrew Jackson, a frontiersman who later became America's seventh president, that he was raising an army to fight the Spanish in order to seize parts of Mexico for the United States. Burr was instead accused of plotting to march on the United States and take Jefferson hostage. He was arrested and brought to trial on charges of treason, but there wasn't enough evidence to prove his guilt.

He lived the remainder of his life as an outcast. Once after reading a tender scene in Laurence Sterne's *Tristram Shandy*, where a kindhearted man releases a fly out the window instead of killing it, Burr reportedly remarked, "Had I read Sterne more and Voltaire less, I should have known the world was wide enough for Hamilton and me."

14

Legacy

uring Alexander Hamilton's lifetime, he was not seen as a visionary or an idealist—Thomas Jefferson, with his pining for an idyllic pastoral America, his penchant for revolutions, and his belief that it was possible to live in a society without taxes, was viewed as the man with the utopian vision. Hamilton was thought of as the practical statesman with a ten-point plan for everything. Thomas Jefferson was often viewed as a humanist and liberal who valued individual liberty above all, while Hamilton was often portrayed as a backward-leaing reactionary who placed law and order above individual freedom, who longed to return to a monarchy, and who embraced the evils of European industry and banking.

But Jefferson, unlike Hamilton, could not imagine blacks and whites living side by side as equals. While Jefferson would have been happy for America to remain a nation of farmers who exchanged raw products for finished goods, Hamilton understood that an economy dependent on others would mean remaining a colony in all but name. Jefferson wanted nothing to do with banks, commerce, industry, or global leadership. Today we can see Hamilton as the farsighted statesman who imagined a capitalistic, multiracial country that would someday belong among the wealthiest and most advanced nations.

Hamilton lived in fear that the country he worked so hard to build would unravel. He worried that the states would pull apart, due process would be denied, and mob rule would prevail. In short, he worried that the American experiment would fail. Indeed, during the centuries since Hamilton's death, there have been times the country nearly came apart. But today—from the skyscrapers of Manhattan, to the interstate highways, to the world's largest and most robust economy overseen by a centralized bank—we are living in Hamilton's America.

Samples of Alexander Hamilton's Work

During the year after Hamilton arrived in New York from the Caribbean, he was a frequent guest in the home of Elias Boudinot. In 1774, when Boudinot's infant daughter died, Hamilton composed this poem for the grieving parents.

"Poem on the Death of Elias Boudinot's Child"

For the sweet babe, my doting heart
Did all a Mother's fondness feel;
Carefull to act each tender part
and guard from every threatening ill.
But what, alas, availed my care?
The unrelenting hand of death,
Regardless of a parent's prayer
Has stoped my lovely Infant's breath—
With rapture number Over thy Charms,

While on thy harmless sports intent,
Or prattling in my happy arms—
No More thy self Important tale
Some embryo meaning shall convey,
Which, should the imperfect accents fail,
Thy speaking looks would still display—
Thou'st gone, forever gone—yet where,
Ah! pleasing thought; to endless bliss.
Then, why Indulge the rising tear?
Canst thou, fond heart, lament for this?
Let reason silence nature's strife,
And weep Maria's fate no more;
She's safe from all the storms of life,
And Wafted to a peaceful Shore.

✳ ✳ ✳ ✳ ✳ ✳ ✳ ✳ ✳ ✳ ✳ ✳ ✳ ✳ ✳

Excerpts from *Federalist Paper* #1, Introduction, as an example of Hamilton's writing and the purpose of the *Federalist Papers*.

To the People of the State of New York:

AFTER an unequivocal experience of the inefficiency of the subsisting federal government, you are called upon to deliberate on a new Constitution for the United States of America. The subject speaks its own importance; comprehending in its consequences nothing less than the existence of the UNION, the safety and welfare of the parts of which it is composed, the fate of an empire in many respects the most interesting in the world. It has been frequently remarked that it seems to have been reserved to the people of this country, by their conduct and example, to decide the important question, whether societies of men are really capable or not of establishing good government from reflection and choice, or whether they are forever destined to depend for their political constitutions on accident and force. If there be any truth in the remark, the crisis at which we are arrived may with propriety be regarded as the era in which that decision is to be made; and a wrong election of the part we shall act may, in this view, deserve to be considered as the general misfortune of mankind. This idea will add the inducements of philanthropy to those of patriotism, to heighten the solicitude which all considerate and good men must feel for the event. Happy will it be if our choice should be directed by a judicious estimate of our true interests, unperplexed and unbiased by considerations not connected with the public good. But this is a thing more ardently to be wished than seriously to be expected. The plan offered to our deliberations affects too many particular interests, innovates upon too many local institutions, not to involve in its discussion a variety of objects foreign to its merits, and of views, passions and prejudices little favorable to the discovery of truth.

Among the most formidable of the obstacles which the new Constitution will have to encounter may readily be distinguished the obvious interest of a certain class of men in every State to resist all changes which may hazard a diminution of the power, emolument, and consequence of the offices they hold under the State establishments; and the perverted ambition of another class of men, who will either hope to aggrandize themselves by the confusions of their country, or will flatter themselves with fairer prospects of elevation from the subdivision of the empire into several partial confederacies than from its union under one government.

I propose, in a series of papers, to discuss the following interesting particulars:

THE UTILITY OF THE UNION TO YOUR POLITICAL PROSPERITY THE INSUFFICIENCY OF THE PRESENT CONFEDERATION TO PRESERVE THAT UNION THE NECESSITY OF A GOVERNMENT AT LEAST EQUALLY ENERGETIC WITH THE ONE PROPOSED, TO THE ATTAINMENT OF THIS OBJECT THE CONFORMITY OF THE PROPOSED CONSTITUTION TO THE TRUE PRINCIPLES OF REPUBLICAN GOVERNMENT ITS ANALOGY TO YOUR OWN STATE CONSTITUTION and lastly, THE ADDITIONAL SECURITY WHICH ITS ADOPTION WILL AFFORD TO THE PRESERVATION OF THAT SPECIES OF GOVERNMENT, TO LIBERTY, AND TO PROPERTY.

In the progress of this discussion I shall endeavor to give a satisfactory answer to all the objections which shall have made their appearance, that may seem to have any claim to your attention.

It may perhaps be thought superfluous to offer arguments to prove the utility of the UNION, a point, no doubt, deeply engraved on the hearts of the great body of the people in every State, and one, which it may be imagined, has no adversaries. But the fact is, that we already hear it whispered in the private circles of those who oppose the new *Constitution*, that the thirteen States are of too great extent for any general system, and that we must of necessity resort to separate confederacies of distinct portions of the whole. This doctrine will, in all probability, be gradually propagated, till it has votaries enough to countenance an open avowal of it. For nothing can be more evident, to those who are able to take an enlarged view of the subject, than the alternative of an adoption of the new Constitution or a dismemberment of the Union. It will therefore be of use to begin by examining the advantages of that Union, the certain evils, and the probable dangers, to which every State will be exposed from its dissolution. This shall accordingly constitute the subject of my next address.

✳ ✳ ✳ ✳ ✳ ✳ ✳ ✳ ✳ ✳ ✳ ✳ ✳ ✳ ✳

One of Alexander Hamilton's letters. Letter writing was the primary means of communication in the eighteenth century. This letter, written after Hamilton left the Continental

Army following his quarrel with General Washington, is to General Greene.

Dear General,

I acknowlege myself to have been unpardonably delinquent in not having written to you before; but my matrimonial occupations have scarcely left me leisure or inclination for any other. I must now be brief as the post is just setting out. I shall shortly write you at large.

I have not been much in the way of knowing sentiments out of the army; but as far as I am acquainted with them either in or out you have great reason to be satisfied; your conduct in the Southern command seems to be universally approved, and your reputation is progressive. How long this will last the wheel of fortune will have too much part in determining.

I cannot tell you anything of our prospects here, because we know little about them ourselves. Hitherto we have received few recruits. I fear this campaign will be a defensive one on our part.

Harrison has left the General to be a Chief Justice

of Maryland. I am about leaving him to be any thing that fortune may cast up. I mean in the military line. This, my dear General, is not an affair of calculation but of feeling. You may divine the rest, and I am sure you will keep your divinations to yourself.

The enemy have gotten so much in the way of intercepting our mails that I am afraid of seeing whatever I write spring up the Week after in Rivingtons Gazette. This obliges me to be cautious. Adieu, My Dear General. Let me beg you will believe that whatever change there may be in my situation there never will be any in my respect, esteem, and affection for you.

A Hamilton

PS. Let me know if I could find any thing worth my while to do in the Southern army. You know I shall hate to be nominally a soldier. General Knox has the confidence of the army & is a man of sense. I think he may be safely made use of. Situated as I am Your Excellency will feel the confidential nature of these observations.

Time Line

1755 ✶ Hamilton was born on the island of Nevis.

1768 ✶ Rachel, Hamilton's mother, died.

1772 ✶ Hamilton left St. Croix for the North American colonies.

1773 ✶ Hamilton began his studies at the Francis Barber Academy.

1774 ✶ Hamilton entered Columbia University.

1776 ✶ Continental Congress declared independence.

   ✶ Hamilton left college to join the New York militia.

1777 ✶ Hamilton became an aide-de-camp to General George Washington.

   ✶ The Articles of Confederation were drafted.

1780 ✶ Hamilton married Eliza Schuyler.

1781 ✶ Hamilton led an attack during the Battle of Yorktown.

1782 ✶ Hamilton passed the New York bar exam and became a lawyer.

   ✶ Hamilton became a continental receiver.

   ✶ Hamilton became a New York delegate to the Continental Congress.

1783 ✶ The Newburgh Conspiracy erupted.

   ✶ The Continental Congress fled to New Jersey in the face of threatened mutiny by soldiers in Pennsylvania.

   ✶ The Treaty of Paris officially ended the Revolutionary War.

Time Line

1784 ✦ Hamilton defended Joshua Waddington in *Rutgers v. Waddington.*

✦ Hamilton founded the Bank of New York.

1786 ✦ Hamilton was elected to the New York legislature.

✦ Maryland and Virginia invited the other states to a convention in Annapolis to address the problems of trade between the states.

✦ Hamilton journeyed to Annapolis as one of New York's delegates.

1787 ✦ The Constitutional Convention convened in Philadelphia.

✦ Hamilton was one of three delegates from New York.

1788 ✦ The new Constitution was ratified.

1789 ✦ George Washington became the nation's first president.

✦ Hamilton became the first secretary of the Treasury.

1791 ✦ Aaron Burr replaced Philip Schuyler as senator from New York.

1797 ✦ President Washington left office.

1797 ✦ John Adams was sworn in as the second president.

1801 ✦ Jefferson became the third president.

✦ Hamilton's son Philip was killed in a duel.

1802 ✦ The Hamiltons moved into their new home, the Grange.

1804 ✦ Hamilton campaigned against Burr's run for the governorship of New York.

✦ Hamilton shot to death in a duel with Burr.

1805 ✦ Thomas Jefferson was sworn in for his second term as president with a new vice president, George Clinton.

Endnotes

Prologue: The Duel

2   "I have resolved . . . reflect": Hamilton, "Statement of Impending Duel with Aaron Burr," June 28–July 10, 1804, http://founders. archives.gov/documents/Hamilton/01-26-02-0001-0241.

2   "Then sir . . . slaughtered": Robert Troup to Timothy Pickering, March 31, 1828, as quoted by Chernow, 691.

3   "If it had been possible . . . best of women": Hamilton to Elizabeth Schuyler, July 4, 1804. http://founders.archives.gov/documents/ Hamilton/01-26-02-0001-0248.

3   "withdraw from the scene . . . made for me": Hamilton to Gouverneur Morris, February 29, 1802, http://founders.archives. gov/documents/Hamilton/01-25-02-0297.

5   "This is a mortal wound, Doctor": David Hosack to William Coleman, August 17, 1804, http://founders.archives.gov/documents/ Hamilton/01-26-02-0001-0280.

1. An Orphan and a Dreamer

6   "My ambition . . . my station": Hamilton to Edward Stevens, November 11, 1769, http://founders.archives.gov/documents/ Hamilton/01-01-02-0002.

16   "I am a youth . . . A.H.": Hamilton to the *Royal Danish American Gazette*, April 6, 1771, http://founders.archives.gov/documents/ Hamilton/01-01-02-0003.

18   "The roaring . . . deliverer": Hamilton to the *Royal Danish American Gazette*, September 6, 1772, http://founders.archives.gov/ documents/Hamilton/01-01-02-0042.

Endnotes

2. An Immigrant

20 "There are . . . to all": Hamilton, *Federalist Paper* #36,
https://www.congress.gov/resources/display/content/
The+Federalist+Papers#TheFederalistPapers-36.

25 I have used the names "Columbia" for King's College in
New York and "Princeton" for King's College in New Jersey,
even though the names weren't changed until after the
Revolution.

26 "enemies to . . . our rights": Hamilton, "A Full Vindication of the
Measures of the Congress," December 15, 1774, http://founders.
archives.gov/documents/Hamilton/01-01-02-0054.

27 "Let it be remembered . . . skill": Hamilton, "The Farmer Refuted,"
February 23, 1775, http://founders.archives.gov/documents/
Hamilton/01-01-02-0057.

27 "lead an honorable . . . death": *New-York Journal* or the *General
Advertiser*, November 23, 1775, as quoted by Chernow, 71.

28 "Death comes . . . stroke": Hamilton to the *Royal Danish American
Gazette*, September 6, 1772.

28 "degenerate . . . race of mortals": Hamilton, "Farmer Refuted."

29–30 "fraud . . . oppression": Mitchell, Broadus. *Alexander Hamilton:
Youth to Maturity.* New York: The Macmillan Company, 1957, 63.

31–32 "In times . . . proper bounds": Hamilton to John Jay,
November 26, 1775, http://founders.archives.gov/documents/
Hamilton/01-01-02-0060.

3. A Soldier

33 "That Americans . . . principle": Hamilton, "Full Vindication."

34 "I am going . . . important cause": Hamilton, "Extract of a Letter
from a Gentleman in New York, Dated February 18th," *Royal Danish
American Gazette*, March 20, 1776, as quoted by Chernow, 72.

Endnotes

38 "the soul of a general": George Washington to James McHenry, July 29, 1798, Papers of the War Department.

38–39 "My time . . . execute orders": George Washington to Lieutenant Colonel Joseph Reed, January 23, 1776, http://founders.archives.gov/documents/Washington/03-03-02-0123.

40 "principal and most confidential aide": George Washington to John Adams, September 25, 1798, http://founders.archives.gov/documents/Washington/06-03-02-0015.

41 "not the least . . . soldiers": Hamilton to John Jay, March 14, 1779, http://press-pubs.uchicago.edu/founders/documents/v1ch15s24.html.

44 "The truth . . . fools and knaves." Hamilton to Lieutenant Colonel John Laurens, September 12, 1780, http://founders.archives.gov/documents/Hamilton/01-02-02-0851.

47 "My heart . . . embarrassments": Hamilton to James Hamilton, June 22, 1785, http://founders.archives.gov/documents/Hamilton/01-03-02-0444.

4. Victory in Love and War

48 "Before no mortal . . . stay": Hamilton to Elizabeth Schuyler, July 2–4, 1780, footnote #2, http://founders.archives.gov/documents/Hamilton/01-02-02-0747.

48 "I give in . . . letters": Washington to the president of Congress, April 23, 1776, as quoted by Mitchell, *Concise Biography*, 42.

49 "Mrs. Washington . . . flag": Rivington's *Gazette*, May 1778, as quoted by Emery, 56.

49 "acquitted himself . . . West Indian": Flexner, James Thomas. *The Young Hamilton*. New York: Fordham University Press, 1997, 149, as quoted by Chernow, 92.

49 "a bright gleam of sunshine": Ibid., 91.

Endnotes

52   "Hamilton's a gone man": Mitchell, *Youth to Maturity*, 198, as
      quoted by Chernow, 128.

54   "I love you . . . your sex": Hamilton to Elizabeth Schuyler,
      July 2–4, 1780.

57   "[T]here are . . . sterling virtue": George Washington to John
      Sullivan, February 4, 1781, http://founders.archives.gov/
      documents/Washington/99-01-02-04754.

57–58 "Colonel Hamilton . . . your choice": Hamilton to Philip
      Schuyler, February 18, 1781, http://founders.archives.gov/
      documents/Hamilton/01-02-02-1089.

58   "I wish . . . in the wrong": Ibid.

59   "Without a shadow . . . disrespect": Hamilton to Major James
      McHenry, February 18, 1781, http://founders.archives.gov/
      documents/Hamilton/01-02-02-1090.

5. Striving for Magnificence

65   "There is something . . . perverse": Hamilton, "The Continentalist,"
      No. VI, *Revolutionary Writings of Alexander Hamilton*, July 4, 1782.

69   "constitutional imbecility": Hamilton, *Works of Alexander
      Hamilton.*

72   "On most occasions . . . soul": Henry Cabot Lodge, as quoted by
      Emery, 87.

74   "The army . . . play with": George Washington to Hamilton,
      April 4, 1783, http://founders.archives.gov/documents/
      Washington/99-01-02-10993.

74   "a civil horror . . . receding": George Washington to Hamilton,
      March 12, 1783, http://founders.archives.gov/documents/
      Hamilton/01-03-02-0179.

74   "not only . . . blind": Washington's Farewell Address of 1796, footnote
      #2.

Endnotes

74 "forced its way . . . eye": *The Journals of Major Samuel Shaw: The First American Consul at Canton (Revolutionary War)*, HardPress Publishing, 2012.

75 "Having no future . . . earnest": Hamilton to George Clinton, May 14, 1783, http://founders.archives.gov/documents/Hamilton/01-03-02-0233.

6. Capitalism: A New Vision for America

77 "'Tis by introducing . . . object": Hamilton to Robert Morris, April 30, 1781, http://founders.archives.gov/documents/Hamilton/01-02-02-1167.

79 "Those who labor . . . God": Robert Leslie to Thomas Jefferson, February 14, 1803, footnote, http://founders.archives.gov/documents/Jefferson/01-39-02-0435.

81 "So light . . . exists": Thomas Jefferson to George Washington, August 14, 1787, http://founders.archives.gov/documents/Jefferson/01-12-02-0040.

82 "There is nothing. . . depravity": Thomas Jefferson to Thomas Cooper, September 10, 1814, http://founders.archives.gov/documents/Jefferson/03-07-02-0471.

82 "bodily coercion": Thomas Jefferson to Thomas Cooper, September 10, 1814, http://founders.archives.gov/documents/Jefferson/03-07-02-0471.

82 "Plan for . . . lack of support": Emery, 82.

83 "Our prospects . . . our errors": Hamilton to John Jay, July 25, 1784. http://founders.archives.gov/documents/Hamilton/01-03-02-0270

7. Due Process of Law

85 "The voice . . . determine right": Robert Yates, *Notes of the Secret*

Debates of the Federal Convention of 1787, http://avalon.law.yale. edu/18th_century/yates.asp.

87 "were by . . . cruelty": Ralph Earl Prime, *George Clinton: Some of His Colonial, Revolutionary, and Post-Revolutionary Services*, https:// archive.org/details/cu31924032753687.

87 "furious and dark passions": Hamilton, "A Letter from Phocion to the Considerate Citizens of New York," January 1–27, 1784, http://founders.archives.gov/documents/Hamilton/01-03-02-0314.

94 "Legislative folly . . . reaping": Hamilton to Gouverneur Morris, February 21, 1784, http://founders.archives.gov/documents/Hamilton/01-03-02-0331.

96 "a commerce . . . enlightened people": "Memorial to Abolish the Slave Trade," March 13, 1786, http://founders.archives.gov/documents/Hamilton/01-03-02-0503.

8. Steps in the Right Direction

97 "Most commercial . . . trade": Hamilton to Robert Morris, April 30, 1781.

100 "present anarchy of our commerce": James Madison to Thomas Jefferson, March 18, 1786, http://founders.archives.gov/documents/Jefferson/01-09-02-0301.

100 "That it is necessary . . . tottering": George Washington to John Jay, May 18, 1786, http://memory.loc.gov/cgi-bin/query/r?ammem/mgw:@field(DOCID+@lit(gw280346)).

102 "all Virginia will be against you": Wills, Garry. *Explaining America: The Federalist*. New York: Penguin Books. 12, as quoted by Chernow, 224.

103 "I hold it . . . government": Thomas Jefferson to James Madison, January 30, 1787, http://www.let.rug.nl/usa/presidents/thomas-jefferson/letters-of-thomas-jefferson/jefl53.php.

Endnotes

9. The Good Ship Hamilton

104 "Why has government . . . constraint": Hamilton, *Federalist Paper* #15, https://www.congress.gov/resources/display/content/The+Federalist+Papers#TheFederalistPapers-15.

107 "elective monarch": Chernow, 234.

109 "I am sorry . . . local views": George Washington to Hamilton, July 10, 1787, http://founders.archives.gov/documents/Washington/04-05-02-0236.

115 "retire to sleep . . . the press": Sullivan, William. *The Public Men of the Revolution*. Philadelphia: Carey and Hart, 1847, 261, as quoted by Chernow, 250.

116 "I never expect . . . man": Hamilton, *Federalist Paper* #85, https://www.congress.gov/resources/display/content/The+Federalist+Papers#TheFederalistPapers-85.

118 "The mighty mind . . . powers": William Kent, *Memoirs and Letters of James Kent* (Boston: Little, Brown and Company, 1898), https://archive.org/stream/memoirslettersofkent/memoirslettersofkent_djvu.txt.

118 "political porcupine, armed at all points": Kline, 200.

121 "Behold . . . share of joy": Gilje and Pencak, 61.

122 "Skin me well . . . fleet": Ibid.

10. Secretary of the Treasury

123 "A national debt . . . blessing": Hamilton to Robert Morris, April 30, 1781.

124–25 This explanation of the Electoral College is from Federalist Paper #68. https://www.congress.gov/resources/display/content/The+Federalist+Papers#TheFederalistPapers-68.

124 "What are we to do . . . Hamilton": McDonald, Forrest. *Alexander*

Endnotes

Hamilton: A Biography. New York: W. W. Norton, 1982 [1979], 128, as quoted by Chernow, 287.

126 "power very unsafe in a republic": Mitchell, *National Adventure*, 15.

129 "the price of liberty": Hamilton, "Report Relative to a Provision for the Support of Public Credit," January 9, 1790, http://founders. archives.gov/documents/Hamilton/01-06-02-0076-0002-0001.

133 "will be a powerful . . . industry": Hamilton to Robert Morris, April 30, 1781.

135 "promote national prosperity": Hamilton, *Report on a National Bank*, as quoted by Ferling, 214.

137 "necessary and expedient": Constitution of the United States, Article II, Section 3.

137 "all laws . . . proper": Constitution of the United States, Article I, Section 8.

139 "carry themselves back": Thomas Jefferson to William Johnson, June 12, 1823, http://founders.archives.gov/documents/ Jefferson/98-01-02-3562.

139 "recollect . . . debates": Thomas Jefferson to William Johnson, June 12, 1823, http://founders.archives.gov/documents/ Jefferson/98-01-02-3562.

11. Rivalry with Jefferson

143 "Tis the malicious . . . harass me": Hamilton to John Jay, December 18, 1792, http://founders.archives.gov/documents/ Hamilton/01-13-02-0169.

144 "The Clintons . . . *Hamilton*": *Aaron Burr: The Years from Princeton to Vice President, 1756– 1805.* New York: Farrar, Straus and Giroux, 1979, 138, as quoted by Chernow, 286.

153 "choice and prudence . . ." and "The name of American . . . local distinctions": Washington's Farewell Address of 1796.

Endnotes

12. Rivalry with Burr

154 "Every day . . . not made for me": Hamilton to Gouverneur Morris, February 29, 1802.

158 "No one . . . extent": Hamilton to Martha Washington, January 12, 1800, http://founders.archives.gov/documents/Hamilton/01-24-02-0140.

159 "Every moment's . . . disgust": Hamilton to Theodore Sedgwick, February 18, 1795, http://founders.archives.gov/documents/Hamilton/01-18-02-0169.

160 "bastard brat of a Scotch peddler": John Adams to Benjamin Rush, January 25, 1806, http://founders.archives.gov/documents/Adams/99-02-02-5119.

161 "is by far . . . character": Hamilton to Oliver Wolcott, Jr., December 16, 1800, http://founders.archives.gov/documents/Hamilton/01-25-02-0131.

162 "We are all. . . Federalists." Lomask, Aaron Burr: The Years from Princeton to Vice President, p. 297, as quoted by Chernow, 640.

165 "lash the rascals": Julius Goebel, Jr., ed., *The Law Practice of Alexander Hamilton* (New York: Columbia University Press, 1964–1981), as quoted by Chernow, 668.

165 "wickedly and maliciously": Mitchell, *National Adventure*, 503.

169 "Mine is an odd destiny . . . fabric": Hamilton to Gouverneur Morris, February 29, 1802.

171 "dishonest . . . public good": Mitchell, *National Adventure*, 525.

171 "Hamilton and Judge Kent . . . government": Charles D. Cooper to Philip Schuyler, April 23, 1804, http://founders.archives.gov/documents/Hamilton/01-26-02-0001-0203-0002.

13. Afterward

175 "Had I . . . Hamilton and me": Fleming, Thomas. *Duel: Alexander Hamilton, Aaron Burr, and the Future of America.* New York: Basic Books, 1999, as quoted by Chernow, 723. (Voltaire was a French philosopher.)

Samples of Alexander Hamilton's Work

178–79 Hamilton, "Poem on the Death of Elias Boudinot's Child," September 4, 1774, http://founders.archives.gov/documents/ Hamilton/01-01-02-0052.

179–83 Hamilton to Major General Nathanael Greene, April 19, 1781, http://founders.archives.gov/documents/Hamilton/01-02-02-1150.

Bibliography

Online Sources

Hamilton's letters and writings are available online. For each Hamilton quotation, I have provided an Internet source so readers can easily access the full content.

The Constitution of the United States: http://www.archives.gov/exhibits/charters/constitution_transcript.html

The Federalist Papers: https://www.congress.gov/resources/display/content/The+Federalist+Papers

Founders' Constitution, University of Chicago Press and the Liberty Fund: http://press-pubs.uchicago.edu/founders

Founders Online, National Archives, Hamilton Papers: http://founders.archives.gov/search/Project%3A%22Hamilton%20Papers%22

Hamilton's letters: http://www.earlyamerica.com/about/

Papers of the War Department, George Mason University: http://wardepartmentpapers.org

Teaching American History, Alexander Hamilton Documents: http://teachingamericanhistory.org/library/hamilton/

Recollections and Private Memoirs of George Washington: https://archive.org/stream/recollectionsan00lossgoog

Washington's Farewell Address of 1796: http://oll.libertyfund.org/pages/1796-george-washington-s-farewell-address-speech

Books

Berkin, Carol. *A Brilliant Solution: Inventing the American Constitution.* Boston: Houghton Mifflin, 2002.

Chernow, Ron. *Alexander Hamilton.* New York: Penguin Publishing Group, 2004. Kindle edition.

Bibliography

Cooke, Jacob E., ed. *Alexander Hamilton: A Profile*. New York: Hill and
Wang, 1967.

Emery, Noemie. *Alexander Hamilton: An Intimate Portrait*. New York: G.P.
Putnam's Sons, 1982.

Gilje, Paul A. and William Pencak, eds. *New York in the Age of the
Constitution, 1775–1800*. Madison, NJ: Fairleigh Dickinson
University Press, 1992.

Ferling, John. *Jefferson and Hamilton: The Rivalry That Forged a Nation*.
New York: Bloomsbury Press, 2013.

Hamilton, Alexander. *The Revolutionary Writings of Alexander Hamilton*.
Edited by Richard B. Vernier. Indianapolis: Liberty Fund, 2008.
http://oll.libertyfund.org/titles/hamilton-the-revolutionary-
writings-of-alexander-hamilton.

——.*The Works of Alexander Hamilton*. Edited by
Henry Cabot Lodge. New York: G.P. Putnam's Sons, 1904.
http://oll.libertyfund.org/titles/hamilton-the-works-of-alexander-
hamilton-federal-edition-12-vols.

Hubbard, Vincent K. *Swords, Ships, and Sugar: History of Nevis to 1900*.
Corvallis, OR: Premiere Editions International, 1998.

Kline, Mary-Jo. *Alexander Hamilton: A Biography in His Own Words*. New
York: Harper & Row, 1973.

Mitchell, Broadus. *Alexander Hamilton: A Concise Biography*. New York:
Barnes and Noble, 1999.

——.*Alexander Hamilton: The National Adventure, 1788–1804*. New
York: Macmillan, 1962.

Acknowledgments

The writing of this book was helped enormously by the unsung heroes of American historical preservation: the many governmental agencies and universities who have taken on the Herculean task of preserving reams of letters and historical records and making them readily available to the public through online searches. These include the National Archives Online Records, the University of Chicago Press and the Liberty Fund, the George Mason University War Papers, and Ashland University's Teaching America site.

Very special thanks to the entire Abrams team: Howard Reeves, an enormously talented editor; the unparalleled Abrams design team, including Sara Corbett and Chad Beckerman, who turned a mere manuscript into a visual work of art; James Armstrong, a sharp, thorough, and sensitive managing editor; Kathy Lovisolo, who guided the book from mere files into a beautiful finished book; Masha Gunic and Orlando Dos Reis, editorial assistants, for keeping together all the bits and pieces; and marketing director Nicole Russo, always such a pleasure to work with. And thanks as always to Betsy Wattenberg and Andy Schloss for their constant support.

Index

Note: Page numbers in *italics* refer to illustrations.

Index